More
Sugar Flowers
for Beginners

Paddi Clark

A step-by-step guide to making beautiful flowers in sugar

My life would never have been the same if it was not for the love, care and great sense of humour shared with my family.

So it is to them that I dedicate this book. To my amazing husband Bruce, who is always steadfast in his support of my undertakings, whether they be projects, sugar sample making or necessary purchases!

Also my sons Oliver, Lawrence and Toby, wherever they may be in the world, for their continued help, encouragement and honest opinions.

And a warm welcome to my first granddaughter, Annabel Lucy, who as she grows hopefully will enjoy 'just a little bit of sugarcraft' maybe!

I wish you all unending happiness. My love as always, and thank you so very much.

First published in March 2012 by B. Dutton Publishing Limited, The Grange, Hones Yard, Farnham, Surrey, GU9 8BB. Copyright: Paddi Clark 2012

ISBN-13: 978-1-905113-26-2

All rights reserved.

No part of this publication may be reproduced, stored in a retrieval system or transmitted in any form or by means electronic, mechanical, photocopying, recording, or otherwise, without prior written permission of the copyright owner. A catalogue record of this book is available from the British Library.

Paddi Clark has asserted her right under the Copyright, Designs and Patents Act, 1988, to be identified as the author of this work.

Publisher: Beverley Dutton
Editor: Jenny Stewart
Art Director/Designer: Sarah Ryan
Deputy Editor: Jenny Royle
Designer: Zena Manicom
Sub Editor/Graphic Designer: Louise Pepé
Editorial Assistant: Amy Norman
PR and Advertising Manager: Natalie Bull
Photography: Alister Thorpe
Printed in China

Acknowledgements

I would like to thank Beverley and Robert Dutton once again for the opportunity to write another book, for which I am most grateful.

This book would not be what it is without the talents of both Jenny Stewart, the editor, who duly proofread and edited my text, and Sarah Ryan, for her artistic flair and design ability on the pages. Thanks to Alister Thorpe for the beautiful photography.

A thank you also to my sisters Jenny and Chrissie, and to Kay and Kirsty for their help and support.

Enormous gratitude to my family, my husband Bruce and sons Oliver, Lawrence and Toby who rallied round with their unending help and encouragement once again.

Thank you to Ryan Wicks of Love Flowers, Rickmansworth who sourced flowers and sample specimens for photographs.

Thank you to you all.

Disclaimer

The Author and Publisher have made every effort to ensure that the contents of this book, if followed carefully, will not cause harm or injury or pose any danger. Please note that some inedible items, such as floral wires and stamens, have been used in the projects in this book. All such inedible items must be removed before the cakes are eaten. Similarly, any non food-grade equipment and substances must not come into contact with any food that is to be eaten. Neither the Author nor the Publisher can be held responsible for errors or omissions and cannot accept liability for injury, damage or loss to persons or property, however it may arise, as a result of acting upon guidelines and information printed in this book.

Foreword

Having been friends with Paddi for over twenty years, it is a pleasure to write a foreword for More Sugar Flowers for Beginners.

Paddi is very dedicated to sugarcraft – not only is her work stunning, she is an absolutely superb tutor. No matter what she is teaching she gives all her knowledge, skills and expertise to her students, whether it's sugar flowers, sugarpaste, royal icing or any other element of the craft.

I am sure this book will inspire many, many people to try sugarcraft for the first time as well as giving avid hobbyists a whole new set of ideas for their sugar floral creations.

Eddie Spence MBE, November 2011

National and international sugarcraft judge and former President of the British Sugarcraft Guild

I was delighted to be asked to write the foreword to this, Paddi Clark's second book, particularly as I was privileged to write the foreword to her first book.

Paddi's skills as a sugar flower maker have long been recognised; with this book she has excelled herself. Crisp, modern design combined with exquisite, delicate flowers requires a fine balance and I feel Paddi has achieved this.

The photography and layout of the book helps the sugarcrafter to see the fine detail and delicacy of Paddi's mastery of this fascinating medium, the popularity of which is growing in leaps and bounds.

The soft, flowing lines of the oriental poppy wedding cake contrast dramatically with the crisp lines of the longiflorum arrangement, demonstrating Paddi's intuitive understanding of shape and form which is absolutely essential in an artist of her calibre.

Anyone who reads or owns this book will be able to further their understanding and mastery of this captivating and exquisite craft.

Tombi Peck, November 2011

Founder Member, British Sugarcraft Guild

Introduction

'Happiness lies in the joy of achievement and the thrill of creative effort.' (Franklin D. Roosevelt)

A powerful but true statement when we embark on something challenging, and achieve it. Hopefully the flowers and projects in this book will do just that!

I designed the book primarily for the beginner or improver, with step-by-step instructions and simple, descriptive text. Some flowers, like the gerbera or peony, may seem daunting but their petals are repetitive to make, so the process is simplified. Other flowers, such as the Matilija poppy, are big and beautiful so only a single bloom used on a cake will give a stunning effect.

Some projects have been made using only single species of flowers and foliage in the arrangement, making the process simple and straightforward. Others show how different flowers and foliage can be brought together to complement each other in an arrangement, ideal if you would like to show off your skills in a more complex display. As with all sugar flowers, they are fragile so do make extra ones, just in case!

Sugar flowers may be time consuming to make, but I always think they are worth the effort, and provide the satisfaction of seeing a beautiful piece of work when finished.

Welcome to my book. Enjoy.

Paddi

Contents

Basic Equipment, Materials and Techniques

Basic Equipment

To complete the projects in this book, you will require the materials and equipment listed here. Whilst some flowers call for specialist items such as particular cutters or veiners, this list covers the basic requirements for all the flowers in this book. I have described the techniques for their use, so if you are new to flower making this should help you get started. The tools are readily available from sugarcraft and cake decorating stockists and there are several manufacturers, so choose whichever works best for you. Make sure you always keep your equipment clean and use solely for sugarcraft projects.

1 Ball or bone tool

These tools come in different forms, depending on the manufacturer. I find a dog bone-shaped tool, whether in metal or plastic, is more useful than the straight variety. This tool is generally used with a foam pad (see no. 11).

Technique
Frilling and softening

Place the leaf or petal onto the pad and roll the ball tool over the edge of the paste, half on the paste and half on the pad. This softens the edges of the paste, removes the cut edge and adds a gentle undulation or more of a defined curl to the leaf or petal, depending on the pressure used. It may take some practice to get the movement correct and achieve the desired effect.

2 CelStick

The CelStick is useful because it has two different shaped ends: a pointed end for creating the centre of flowers and a rounded end, which can be used to open the flower centre wider if required. It can also be used as a small

rolling pin. Available in small, medium and large sizes, I find the medium size is the most useful for sugar flowers.

3 Cocktail sticks

Cocktail sticks are an important part of the tool kit. They are useful for adding colour to flower paste: dip the tip into the paste colour and mix it into the flower paste. This helps to control the amount of colour used. They are also used to frill the edges of flowers and sugarpaste. To use a cocktail stick to support the flower or bud if it is to be made as an unwired piece, dip the stick into white vegetable fat and then push it into the sugar. Once the flower/bud is dry, twist to remove it.

4 Cotton thread

Fine, cotton thread can be used for making bunches of stamens when a large number is required. White thread can be dusted with any food colour to make the correct shade and, as black stamens are fairly common, it is also useful to keep black thread to hand for this purpose.

5 Craft knife
(or small, sharp knife)

Use a craft knife to trim the paste where necessary and cut out freehand shapes. It is advisable not to do this when the paste is on the rolling board as you may damage the surface of the board.

6 Cutters
(or templates)

There are cutters available for most types of flowers and leaves and many manufacturers make different kinds. They make recreating a leaf or flower

quick and easy, particularly when used in conjunction with the corresponding veiner (see no. 14). If you don't have a particular cutter you can make your own template using a real leaf or flower pressed in a book to flatten it. Draw the shape onto paper, cardboard or acetate, and always write the species on it. It is important to remember that some flowers and leaves are poisonous and must not come into direct contact with edible items.

7 Cutting wheel
(plain edge)

This multipurpose tool has a large wheel at one end and a small wheel at the other. It is very useful in sugar floristry for cutting out petals and leaves, either when using templates or cutting freehand. It is also excellent for cutting other roll-out sugar pastes that you may use in cake decorating.

8 Floral tape

Floral tape (also known as floristry tape and flower tape) has a papery matt surface and is used to cover wire stems and add in flowers and leaves to stems and branches. There are many different colours to choose from but the most frequently used in sugar floristry are the natural shades, like light and dark green, white, beige, and brown.

Technique

Using floral tape

First cut a length of tape then cut this to the width required either in a tape shredder or with scissors (see below). Always stretch the tape to release the glue before taping the stem.

Top tip

It is not always advisable to tape down the whole length of each wire if the leaf or flower is to be attached to a spray or leaf formation as it makes the arrangement very thick and bulky. Instead, start underneath the flower or leaf and wind ¼-width (or finer) floral tape down the wire to the point where the individual stem will be joined to the main stem. Add the next piece into the spray and continue to tape down both wires. Repeat this process until all the leaves and flowers have been added into the spray. The exception to this rule is when you are taping the stems of individual flowers that require a very thick stem. In this case, you need to tape down the entire stem.

9 Floral tape shredder

This is a small machine into which floral tape is inserted and then pulled through across razor blades, which cut it into the required width. The tape can be used as full-width, or cut to ½-width or ¼-width, depending on the item to be taped. If you don't have a tape shredder, wind the length of tape over two fingers neatly and then cut to the required width using sharp scissors.

10 Floral wires

Wires (also known as floristry wires) are used to give petals and leaves extra support. They come in a variety of gauges (widths) – the higher the gauge number, the finer the wire (e.g. 30-gauge is a thinner wire than 24-gauge). The gauge you require will depend on the size of the petal or leaf you are making (i.e. large petals need more support and therefore thicker or lower-gauge wires). Wires are also available in a range of different colours but I tend to use white when wiring a petal or a pale leaf and green for the darker leaves so that the wire is not as visible in the finished piece. There are several methods for wiring petals and leaves: full instructions are given on pages 19 to 22.

11 Foam pad

This is a firm, food-grade pad that softens when pressure is applied to the surface. It is used in conjunction with a ball/bone tool to thin and soften the edges of petals and leaves (see ball tool, above), making them look more realistic.

12 Glass-headed pins

These are used to mark a design/pattern onto sugar, and to hold ribbon in position before it is attached around the cake or board. Always use glass-headed pins so they can be seen easily, sterilise them before use and make sure you remove the pins and store them safely after use.

13 Kitchen roll

This is used when dusting flowers and leaves to remove the excess dust colour from the brush. You have more control when there is less dust on the brush, giving a smoother application onto the sugar.

14 Leaf and petal veiners

There is a vast range of veiners available for creating a huge array of petal and leaf varieties and most brands can be purchased from sugarcraft shops. I find that double-sided veiners are best for creating the most realistic finish as they emboss veins on the front and back of the petal or leaf at the same time.

15 Non-slip mat

This is very useful underneath cake boards and boxes when transporting cakes or flowers to hold them safely in place. As sugar flowers are very delicate, protect them with bubble wrap or kitchen roll when transporting them. A non-slip mat can also be placed under a rolling board (see below) to prevent it from slipping on the work surface.

16 Non-stick rolling board

This is an essential piece of equipment for making sugar flowers and once you have one, it should last for years. They are available in different sizes: larger ones are ideal for use when covering cakes and smaller ones are better for

sugar flowers. They are produced in several colours (depending on the manufacturer) – I would recommend using a coloured board rather than a white one, as it is more restful on the eyes. Some boards have grooves within them to create ridges in the paste for the wired petals and leaves; this type of board can also be turned over and used as a flat, non-stick surface.

To take care of your board, keep it clean and never use a craft knife on the surface as it can score the board and damage it.

17 Non-stick rolling pin

A small, non-stick, polypropylene rolling pin is an essential piece of equipment for rolling paste smooth and thin. Rolling pins are available in different sizes but a medium size (around 23cm/9") is probably the most useful for flower making.

18 Paintbrushes

It is advisable to have a selection of good quality, man-made bristle brushes to hand when making sugar flowers, as these produce the best effects when dusting colour onto petals and leaves. Different sized brushes are available; I frequently use nos. 5 to 10 flat brushes and nos. 00 to 4 round brushes. Both

types of brush have their uses: flat brushes are more efficient for dusting large areas while round brushes will reach into smaller areas of the flower (e.g. the centre) and are better suited for painting on fine detail such as spots and lines.

19 Paint palette

A plastic palette is useful for mixing dust colours in order to achieve the correct colour for the flowers or leaves you are making. You can also use the palette to mix the dust colour with glaze cleaner, clear alcohol or water to make a paint.

20 Paperclips

A few of these should be kept available for use to place under polystyrene formers or apple trays to hold them in place whilst the flowers are drying.

21 Photographer's air blower (not pictured)

I use an air blower made for cleaning camera lenses to remove any unwanted specs of florist dust from flowers, leaves and covered cakes. Alternatively you can use a clean, empty squeeze bottle. Never blow on sugar pieces as it is unhygienic.

22 Pointed tweezers or pliers

It is worth investing in a pair of long, pointed tweezers or pliers and also a pair with curved ends. Both are useful for holding and moving flowers once they have been taped in place as they can get to places where fingers will not reach!

23 Polystyrene bud shapes (not pictured)

These can be wired then covered in flower paste and used as the centre for roses and other large flowers. This prevents the bud from becoming too heavy on the wire.

24 Polystyrene dummies (not pictured)

These are made in many different sizes and shapes and are used for sugarcraft displays and for sample purposes. They are a great way to add extra tiers to wedding cakes where no more cake is required.

25 Polystyrene formers

Cup-shaped formers are available in various sizes and are ideal for drying and shaping petals and leaves. Apple trays from the supermarket are also useful, particularly if you are drying a large number of petals or leaves. You can also use kitchen foil made into cup shapes, or rings of kitchen roll as formers.

26 Polythene bags
(not pictured)

To avoid paste drying out while it is not being used, seal it in a food-grade polythene bag and it will retain its moisture.

27 Posy picks

For hygiene and safety reasons, floral wire should never be inserted directly into a cake. Instead, insert the ends of wired flowers and leaves into a posy pick filled with sugarpaste and then position this on the cake top. It is essential to remove all wired decorations from the cake before cutting it; using a posy pick makes this safe and easy to do.

28 PVA glue
(not pictured)

Use a non-toxic craft glue such as PVA for sticking wire, stamens and floral tape together. Although this glue is non-toxic, it should not come into direct contact with items that are intended for consumption as it is not an edible or food-grade product.

29 Rose wire

This can be used if there are many flowers in the spray and the floral tape is not strong enough to hold them. It also helps to tighten the flower stems so that they hold together more firmly. To use it, place the wire underneath the spray, wind it around the stems and pull tight, taking care not to snap the flowers.

30 Scriber

A scriber (sometimes called a needle tool or scribing needle) is a tool that is used for scratching or pricking a design on a cake. A scriber is also useful for moving wires in a flower spray where fingers will not reach.

31 Silk veining/texturing tool

Available in either plastic or ceramic material, silk veining tools can be rolled over the surface of petals and leaves to add texture. Among other cake decorating uses, they are an ideal tool for frilling petal edges when a slightly rough effect is required.

32 Small palette knife

A small palette knife is an essential piece of equipment for making sugar flowers. They are available in different sizes, from very small to a medium size, either as a cranked or straight version. Use whichever you find most comfortable; I tend to use a tiny one, also known as a Kemper tool.

33 Small, pointed scissors

These are often used to cut the edges of calyces and petals from templates and to tidy up edges if required. The finer the point of the scissors (i.e. the narrower the tips), the easier they are to use.

34 Stamens

There are several varieties of stamens available, but in general small, round stamens, seed-headed matt stamens and very fine ones are the most useful. They also come in different colours, but white ones are the most versatile

as these can be coloured with dust or painted with food colour.

35 Stay Soft flower base

An inedible product with similar properties to Plasticine, Stay Soft is used by florists in flower arranging (it can be purchased at some garden centres and florists). The stems of flowers can be inserted as many times as necessary until the desired arrangement has been achieved. Sugar florists can use Stay Soft for the same purpose if the flowers are for a keepsake: they should be placed in a container and never directly onto a cake. If the display is for a cake, use firm pastillage as an alternative.

36 Tin foil

This is useful to use as a former for flowers or as an instant palette or holder for pollen grains.

37 Veining (Dresden) tool

The thin end of this tool is used for veining the centre of leaves and petals and can also be used for cutting a serrated edge on leaves. The broad end is used to soften and flatten the edges and also flute them. The final result is different to the effect that is created with a ball tool.

38 Wire cutters

A small pair of wire cutters is essential for cutting floral wires to the required length.

Materials

Important Note: Although sugar flowers are made, for the most part, from edible products this is only to ensure they are hygienically safe for display on top of celebration cakes. Never consume sugar flowers if they are made with other items that are inedible, e.g. wire, stamens and inedible glazes. If you are making flowers for a cake, always remove them from the cake top before the cake is cut.

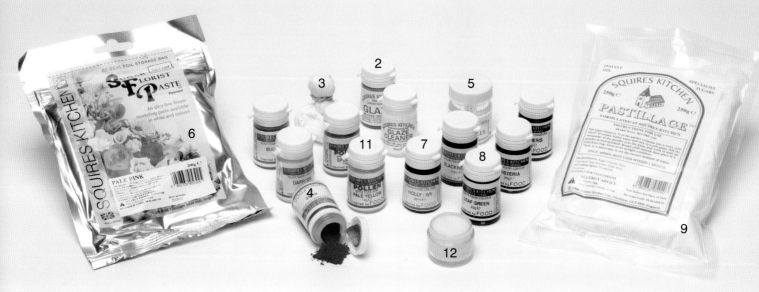

1 CMC/gum tragacanth
(not pictured)

CMC and gum tragacanth are both gums that are used for strengthening sugarpaste (e.g. when making drapes), flower paste and other similar mediums. If you are colouring paste a deep colour you may find that it becomes too soft, so CMC or gum tragacanth can be used to counteract this. Both are available from sugarcraft suppliers (see page 176).

2 Confectioner's glaze/ varnish and glaze cleaner (IPA)*

At full-strength, confectioners' glaze creates a strong, permanent varnished effect when applied to a sugar surface. Often, this can be too shiny to resemble the natural look of some petals and leaves so it is advisable to dilute the confectioners' glaze to ½- or ¼-strength with clear alcohol (such as gin or vodka) or glaze cleaner (see below). There is a glaze spray on the market but this should be used outdoors, following the manufacturer's instructions.

Glaze cleaner (also known as isopropyl alcohol or IPA) is used alongside the glaze to clean brushes and any spills. It can be mixed with dust colours to create a quick-drying food paint (see below), as well as for diluting the glaze.

*Please note that glaze cleaner is an inedible product and should only be used on pieces that will not be eaten.

Technique
Glazing a leaf or petal

The easiest way to glaze a leaf or petal is to transfer the confectioners' glaze into an open-necked jar and dip the pieces into it, holding the end of the floristry wire to which the petal or leaf is attached. Lift the piece out of the glaze but keep it in the jar while you slowly spin the leaf or petal to remove any excess glaze. Hang it to dry on a flower stand or similar. Do not touch the leaf or petal until the glaze has completely dried.

3 Cornflour/cornstarch

Cornflour has several uses in flower making: it can be dusted onto the rolling board to prevent the flower paste from sticking; it can be mixed with flower paste to regain the correct consistency if it becomes too tacky (e.g. after adding a lot of paste food colour); and it can also be used to clean paintbrushes after they have been used for dusting – simply dip the bristles into the cornflour then rub them onto kitchen paper to remove the dust food colour.

To make a cornflour duster place a spoonful of cornflour into a square of muslin or another fine material, fold up the corners and tie with a rubber band. Use this to dust the work board and prevent the paste from sticking.

4 Dust food colours

Edible dust colours are ideal for enhancing the colour of your sugar flowers or leaves and there is a wonderful range of colours available from a number of manufacturers. Throughout this book, I have used Squires Kitchen's Professional Dust Food Colours.

Technique
Colouring petals and leaves

Always use dust food colours sparingly. After dipping a dry, flat paintbrush into the dust, rub the bristles on a piece of kitchen towel to remove the excess colour: this will give you more control when you apply the dust to the sugar surface. Once you have achieved the desired colour, you may wish to pass the petal or leaf through the steam from a boiling kettle to set the colour and give a slightly shiny appearance. Allow to dry.

Technique
Painting with Dust Colours

To apply dust colours in a specific area, a quick-drying, edible paint can be made by mixing the dust with glaze cleaner (IPA). As soon as it is dry the colour will become a powder again (and will rub off), so pass it through steam to set the colour on the sugar. Liquid and paste food colours mixed with cooled, boiled water can also be used for surface painting; the effects are different with all three.

Top tips

• Catching the edges of flowers or leaves with a slightly darker colour than the paste is a particularly effective way of enhancing the colour.

• To lighten darker shades of dust food colour, mix them with white (Edelweiss) dust colour. (Cornflour can also be used for the same purpose but the result is not as effective.)

• As more dust colour is brushed onto a flower or leaf, you will notice the paste will eventually stop absorbing the colour. When this happens, carefully pass the flower or leaf through the steam from a boiling kettle. Once it dries, you can apply more dust colour and the paste will absorb it again. Remember that steam can scald, so always take care when steaming flowers and leaves. Do not steam them for too long otherwise the sugar will dissolve.

5 Edible glue

Edible glue (or sugar glue) is used to stick pieces of sugar work together. It can be purchased ready-made from your local sugarcraft shop or you can make your own using the following recipe:

Dissolve 5ml (1tsp) of gum tragacanth in 15ml (3tsp) of cooled, boiled water. You can alter the consistency if necessary by adding more water. Store the sugar glue in a small, sterilised pot or jar.

Stronger edible glue for larger repairs can be made by 'letting down' some flower paste with edible glue or cooled, boiled water. Adding the water or glue to the paste and working it through well will create a thick, tacky consistency. To ensure the strong edible glue blends into the colour of the piece you are repairing, retain some coloured flower paste for this purpose.

6 Flower paste/Sugar Florist Paste/gum paste

There are many ready-to-use flower pastes on the market, such as Squires Kitchen's Sugar Florist Paste (SFP). Because it is ready-made, the recipe is always consistent and therefore more convenient to use. It also comes in many colours, which is a real time-saver. However, if you would rather make your own flower paste, I have included a recipe below. The ingredient quantities can be adjusted if necessary (e.g. if the paste is too soft, add a little more gum tragacanth to stiffen the paste) and colour can be added before use if required (see paste food colours on page 14). This recipe can also be frozen for later use: simply separate it into smaller amounts and seal in an airtight, food-grade freezer bag.

Top tip

Flower paste should always be sealed in a food-grade polythene bag when not in use, otherwise it will dry out.

Flower paste recipe

450g (1lb) icing/confectioners' sugar

15ml (1 level tbsp) gum tragacanth

30ml (2tbsp) cooled, boiled water

14ml (2 heaped tsp) gelatine

20ml (4tsp) white vegetable fat

1 x size one 'Lion Quality' egg – white only, discard the yolk

10ml (2tsp) liquid glucose

Method

1 Place the icing sugar in an ovenproof bowl. Turn on the oven to a low heat and place the bowl into the oven for a few minutes to warm the sugar.

2 Pour the cooled, boiled water into a bowl and sprinkle the gelatine on top. Leave to soak for 10 minutes.

3 Warm the gelatine and water in the microwave or a bain-marie to dissolve the gelatine completely. Ensure the mixture does not boil.

4 Add the liquid glucose and white vegetable fat to the gelatine mixture and stir. Set aside to allow the ingredients to dissolve.

5 Gently beat the egg white (do not whisk) then add this, the gum tragacanth and the gelatine mixture to the icing

Top tip

Dip the spoon in cooled, boiled water before you dip it into the liquid glucose as this will ensure the glucose slides off the spoon into the mixture more easily.

Important Note: The Food Standards Agency recommends using only pasteurised egg in any food that will not be cooked (or only lightly cooked).

If you decide to use fresh egg white always use eggs bearing the Lion mark, which guarantees that they have been produced to the highest standards of food safety. All Lion Quality eggs come from British hens vaccinated against salmonella, are fully traceable and have a 'best before' date on the shell as a guarantee of freshness.

Eggs can carry bacteria, so always wash your hands before and after handling eggshells. Cracked or dirty eggs should not be used. Good hygiene should always be practised when preparing any food. For more information and advice, contact the Food Standards Agency or the British Egg Information Service.

sugar in the warmed bowl. Mix with a warmed beater on a slow speed until all the ingredients have combined. Increase the speed and beat the mixture until it forms a stringy texture (approximately seven minutes).

6 Remove the mixture from the bowl and knead in some more white vegetable fat if required. Cover the surface of the paste with a layer of white vegetable fat then place it in a food-grade polythene bag and seal in an airtight container. Leave the container in the refrigerator for approximately eight to 12 hours to allow the paste to mature.

7 The paste will set hard. Break or cut the required amount off the bulk of the paste then knead it to soften. Rub some white vegetable fat onto your fingertips to aid this process.

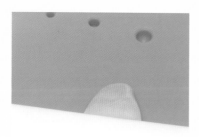

Top tip

If the paste dries out whilst you are using it, dip your fingers into cooled, boiled water and knead the water into the paste to soften it. If this makes the paste too sticky, knead in some white vegetable fat.

Technique

Working with flower paste

Smear some white vegetable fat onto the surface of the rolling board then roll out the flower paste. To check the paste is at the correct thickness for petals and leaves, place it over a sheet of printed lettering. If you can see the lettering through the paste then it is thin enough to work with. Lift the paste and turn it over, then lay it onto a clean work surface (with no white vegetable fat) and cut out the leaf or petal shape you require.

7 Liquid food colours

Use these for painting dots, lines and other markings onto the flowers and leaves. Liquid colours have a stronger effect than dust colours.

8 Paste food colours

These can be used to colour the flower paste, but do start with a small amount of colour first as it can be strong. Use a cocktail stick to remove the colour from the pot, add this to the paste and knead well. If dark/strong colours are required it can make the paste sticky so the powdered dusts can be used in conjunction with paste colours to counteract this. Leave the paste for a while for the colour to mature.

9 Pastillage

If you are making a floral display for a cake, use a firm ball of pastillage to hold the wires in place (rather than Stay Soft). Never push wires directly into any part of the cake that is to be eaten.

Pastillage recipe

10g (approx. 1tsp) gum tragacanth/ CMC powder

170g (6oz) royal icing

85g (3oz) icing/confectioners' sugar

Method

Mix the gum into the royal icing, add the icing sugar and knead well. Place it into a food-grade polythene bag. Add more icing sugar for a firmer consistency.

It is important that the pastillage is covered at all times as it dries out quickly when exposed to the air.

10 Piping gel
(not pictured)

A clear, edible gel that can be used for a number of decorative purposes such as creating dewdrops on leaves and petals.

11 Pollen-style dust food colours

Edible pollen-style dusts are available in a range of ready-made colours from sugarcraft suppliers: these are quick and easy to use. You can also make your own by mixing dust food colour with fine semolina.

12 White vegetable fat

This is used to grease the non-stick board you are working on to prevent the paste from sticking to it. Simply smear a small amount onto the board with your fingertips. It can also be used to soften the paste if it dries out: rub a little into the palms of your hands and knead it into the paste.

Flower Parts

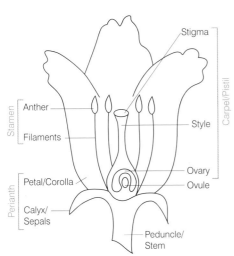

Making Flowers and Leaves

Each individual flower and leaf has its own specific instructions, though there are several techniques that are common in flower making. The terminology and methods are described here, giving an easy reference for many of the flowers and leaves in this book.

Basic Equipment and Edibles

A full description of the edibles and equipment that are used in making sugar flowers is given on pages 6 to 15. However, this list of the basic items can be used as a quick reference before you start. Additional items required for each specific project are given in the equipment and edibles list at the beginning of each one.

Basic Edibles

Cornflour

Dust food colours (SK) (refer to project for specific colours)

Edible glue (SK)

Paste food colours (SK) (refer to project for specific colours)

Sugar Florist Paste (SK) (refer to project for specific colours)

White vegetable fat

Basic Equipment

Ball/bone tool

CelStick

Cocktail sticks

Craft knife

Cutters for the flowers and leaves (refer to project for specific cutters)

Cutting wheel

Dresden tool

Floral tape (refer to project for specific colours)

Floral wires (refer to project for specific colours and gauges)

Foam pad

Food-grade polythene bags

Former (such as tin foil or an apple tray)

Non-stick board

Non-stick rolling pin

Paintbrushes: round and flat (SK)

Polythene bags

PVA glue

Scriber

Silk veining tool

Small palette knife

Small pliers

Small scissors

Stamens (if required, refer to project)

Wire cutters

Flower Making Techniques

Mexican hat

The Mexican hat technique is used to make the basic shape for small flowers like blossoms and calyces for larger flowers.

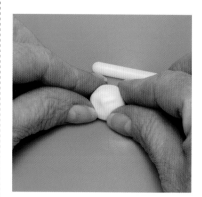

1 Shape a ball of flower paste into a cone.

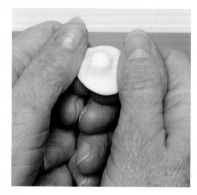

2 Flatten and pinch out the edges of the large end to flatten the paste.

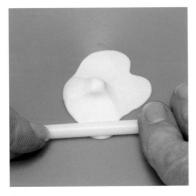

3 Stand the cone on a rolling board greased with white vegetable fat and thin the edges of the large end by rolling a CelStick from the middle outwards.

4 Place the required cutter over the cone and press out the shape. Lift the cone at the narrow end and turn it flower-side up.

5 Use the pointed end of a CelStick to open the centre of the flower/calyx then widen the indentation with the rounded end.

Cupping

Cupping petals gives them a natural curve, as if they have opened out from the flower centre.

1 Place the flower or petal on a foam pad or in the palm of your hand.

2 Soften or shape each petal by gently rolling a bone/ball tool in the centre, causing the paste to form a cup shape.

3 If the petal needs extra curl, place the bone/ball tool on the tip of each petal and gently press towards the centre to make the petal curl in further.

Ski stick

The 'ski stick' is used for creating centres of flowers that are particularly large or flat, e.g. the daisy.

1 Hold the end of a length of floral wire with a pair of fine pliers, then wrap the wire around the tip of the pliers to form a loop.

2 Remove the pliers and flatten the loop flush against the length of the wire.

3 With the pliers, hold the straight length of wire at the central point of the loop. Bend this point back 90° so that the loop of wire sits horizontally on top of the straight piece of wire, thus forming a 'ski stick' shape.

'T' bar

This shape is sometimes used to create large stamens, such as in the Longiflorum lily.

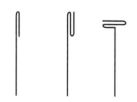

1 Bend a length of floral wire over on itself no more than 5mm (¹/₈") from the end of the wire. Bend the wire again by another 5mm (¹/₈").

2 Hold this with the pliers then pull the long end back to the middle to form a long 'T' shape.

Cage

This can be used as a way to mark grooves evenly into the paste when making larger buds, e.g. lilies.

1 Cut two 26-gauge wires into thirds. Tape five of the wires together firmly at one end.

2 Wire the bud you need and shape as required, then place the bud point-down into the wire cage. Arrange the wires around it evenly then press and squeeze the wires at the top into the soft sugar.

Microwave flower press and laminator

It is a good idea to preserve real flowers and leaves so you can refer to them, even when they are out of season. The make-up of the flower is permanent, so you can see the number of stamens, shape of the petals and veining.

1 Section the flower/leaves in sequence of their growth pattern and then use a microwave press in accordance with the instructions (or press them using the traditional method).

2 Put the dried flowers through a laminator to preserve them: ensure you open out all the petals to expose the detail in the centre of the flower and make sure the calyx at the back of the flower is unfolded.

Top tip

Even after lamination, you will find that the natural colours of some specimens still fade over time, so back them up with photographs.

Making Wired Leaves

Leaves are a very important element of floral displays – they enhance and complement flowers and can even look stunning in an arrangement all on their own, showing off their varying shapes and colours.

There are several methods used for making leaves (which can also be used for petals). When you are new to a craft, I always think it is a good idea to know your options and decide on the method that works best for you.

Whichever method you choose, it is always worth remembering a few basic guidelines:

• Always make spare leaves and petals to allow for breakages before you have completed the project.

• Only use a small amount of flower paste at any one time; you will find it goes a long way and will dry out if it is exposed to the air and not being used.

• Once the paste has been rolled out, lift it with a palette knife and turn it over onto a non-greased area before cutting out the shape required.

• When using a cutter, ensure you press it onto the paste firmly and jiggle the cutter on the board before pulling the paste away and lifting off the cutter. This will guarantee a clean cut.

• If you are left with a rough edge once the petal or leaf is dry, gently file it away with a soft emery board (kept for sugarcraft use only).

Method 1: Using a grooved board

Basic edibles and equipment (see page 16)

1 Cut a floral wire to the required length.

2 Colour the SFP as required.

3 Grease a grooved, non-stick board with a little white vegetable fat.

4 Roll out a small amount of SFP over a groove on the board.

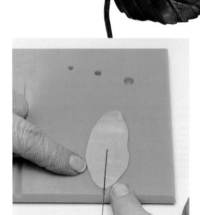

5 Glue a piece of wire, just enough to make it tacky.

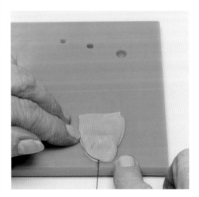

6 Place the wire on top of the paste, over the groove. Fold the top of the paste over to cover the wire and roll over it again, making sure that you use enough pressure to stick the paste to the wire.

7 Cut out the leaf using the relevant cutter. Gently free the shape from the board with a palette knife, starting at the base.

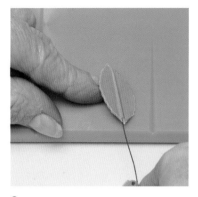

8 Place the leaf into a veiner and press gently to vein the leaf.

9 If required, place the leaf back on the board and softly frill the edges with a silk veining tool.

10 Allow the leaf to semi-dry on some crumpled kitchen paper then dust as required.

11 Make further leaves in varying sizes following the same method. Tape each wire with floral tape then tape these into a stem, as required.

Top tip

If the leaves are very small, turn the board around so you are using it upside down and roll out the paste over the thinner part of the groove.

Method 2: Sausage of paste on a wire

Basic edibles and equipment (see page 16)

1 Cut a floral wire to the required length.

2 Colour the SFP as required.

3 Roll a small sausage of SFP and gently insert a wire through the middle in a twisting motion.

4 Grease a non-stick board with a little white vegetable fat. Place the wired paste onto the board and roll over it with a rolling pin.

5 When the wire is just visible, roll a CelStick outwards from the centre to the edges of the paste on both sides of the wire. Roll over the tip of the leaf away from the top of the wire, leaving a ridge down the centre.

6 Cut out the leaf shape using the required cutter.

7 Place the leaf onto a foam pad and gently soften the edges of the leaf with a bone/ball tool. Use the bone/ball tool again to stretch the edges at the top.

8 Vein the leaf in the relevant veiner then soften the edges again with the bone/ball tool.

9 Repeat the process to make leaves of varying sizes, then dust and tape the leaves as required.

Method 3: Thin paste on a wire

Basic edibles and equipment (see page 16)

1 Cut a floral wire to the required length.

2 Colour the SFP as required.

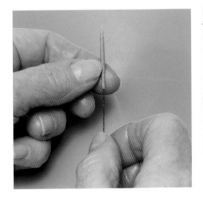

3 Roll a tiny ball of SFP and insert a length of wire into the ball. Roll the paste down the wire on a foam pad to form a very thin covering at one end.

4 Make several of these and place them into a food-grade polythene bag to prevent the paste from drying out.

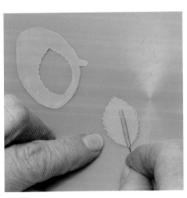

5 Roll out the rest of the SFP on a rolling board lightly greased with white vegetable fat. Cut out a leaf shape using your chosen cutter.

6 Place the leaf on a foam pad and use a ball tool to gently undulate and soften the edges.

7 Position the leaf shape on the half of the veiner that has the raised central vein pattern. Place the wired paste

halfway down the centre of the leaf shape then press the other half of the veiner on top of this. When the veiner is removed, the wire will have merged into the back of the leaf.

8 Allow the leaf to semi-dry then dust as required.

9 Make further leaves following the same method. Tape each wire with floral tape then tape these into a stem, as required.

Method 4: Wiring a completed leaf

Basic edibles and equipment (see page 16)

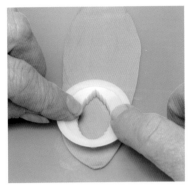

1 Grease a rolling board with white vegetable fat. Roll out some SFP in your chosen colour and cut out a leaf shape using the required cutter.

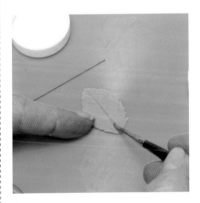

2 Use a veiner to emboss the vein pattern on the leaf surface then soften the edges with a bone/ball tool on a foam pad.

3 Cut a floral wire to the required length. Apply a little edible glue to approximately 1cm (½") of wire at one end, making it only slightly tacky (this is very important as the glue will resist dust colour). Position this on the top surface of the leaf in the centre.

4 Lift one half of the paste and fold the leaf in half, laying one side of the paste on top of the other. Very gently press the back surface of the paste near the wire (if you press too hard the two sides of the leaf will stick together) then set aside for approximately two or three minutes. Continue to make more leaves, following the previous steps, while you wait.

5 Open the folded leaf. The wire should now be covered within the ridge created down the centre.

6 Soften the leaf with a bone/ball tool for a more natural look then dust as required.

7 Make several leaves in varying sizes and tape to a stem using floral tape.

Method 5: Floral tape leaves

Basic edibles and equipment (see page 16)

1 Cut off a piece of floral tape to the required length, depending on the leaf being made. Stretch the tape to release the glue.

2 Brush PVA glue to halfway along the tape on the sticky surface.

3 Place a floral wire halfway up along the length of tape then fold the tape over it with the wire down the centre. Press down along the length of the tape and wire then leave this to dry completely.

4 Using a sharp pair of scissors, cut down one side of the wire from the tip towards the base to shape the leaf then repeat on the other side. Cut the tip to a point.

5 Repeat the above steps to create more leaves in different sizes.

6 Brush the surface of the leaves with dust food colour if required.

Top tip

Grasses such as the Phoenix palm are perfectly suited to this method, but any tiny leaves or indeed long, thin ones such as daffodil leaves can be made using this method.

Top tips

- Make a hole in the centre of a small square of foam sponge. Push the handle of your glue brush through the hole to hold it when not in use.

- When pushing a wire into a sausage of paste (see Method 2 for making leaves) hold the wire at the end and use a twisting/drilling motion to ease it into the paste. The wire should go up through the middle of the paste.

- If, when softening the edges of a petal or leaf with a ball tool, you get a thick ridge on the inside of the paste, it means that you have rolled out the paste too thick. Roll over the paste again with a rolling pin then vein and soften as required.

- When using floral tape, cut less than you think may be needed as small lengths are easier to work with. Make sure you stretch the tape being used to release the glue so that it sticks to itself (stretching it will almost double the length of the tape).

- When using flower paste, always make sure that it is kneaded and worked well to soften it.

- Transporting sugar flowers can be a problem because they are so fragile. Make sure the vase or container is stable and stuck down in the box. Carefully put pieces of facial tissue, bubble wrap or something soft between the flowers that might knock together whilst travelling. Take extra care when doing this to avoid breaking the petals and leaves. Do not use cotton wool or any fibrous material which might catch and stick to the petals.

- When making several petals for one flower, place the petals you have made into a large polythene bag to prevent them from drying too fast. Once all the petals are made they may have to be left out of the bag for a short while before assembly so that they are firm enough to hold their shape. This also applies to leaves.

- When using cutters you can sometimes find a 'furry' edge around the petal, flower or leaf shape. To remove this, make sure that you jiggle the cutter on the board first; if the paste stays in the cutter, turn it over and run your finger over the surface to neaten the edge.

- Occasionally large flowers such as lilies may need extra support whilst drying. Form a piece of foil into the required support shape (a cone or cup shape), make the wired petal and push the wire through the foil. Hold it in place with a paper clip below the flower head until it has hardened enough to hold its shape.

- When sticking pieces together it is important that very little sugar glue is used on the brush, otherwise the paste will become slippery and messy and take longer to stick. Make sure there is no glue on areas of the flower to be dusted as the glue will resist dust colour.

- When making white or very pale flowers, it is advisable to wash your hands frequently – it is amazing how soon the paste becomes grey! Don't forget to wipe the board and rolling pin clean, too.

- It is important to assemble flowers and leaves whilst they are semi-dry as they are still flexible and more likely to fit together better. If they do dry out before assembly, hold them over the steam from a kettle to soften them again, allow the surface moisture to dry then reshape and arrange them as necessary. Do not steam them for too long otherwise the sugar will dissolve.

Simple Wiring and Arrangements

Before you start to assemble an arrangement, make sure you have completed all the required flowers and leaves plus a few extra ones in case of breakages. If you do not use the extra pieces on this occasion, you can always keep them between sheets of kitchen roll, bubble wrap or tissue paper and store them in a cardboard box for later use.

I have used the same flowers in the samples here to show in a simple way the different shapes and styles of floral arrangements and the methodology to create them. The same ideas can be used with any other flowers and leaves.

The flowers used here are:

1 large white rose

3 small white rose buds

Rose leaves

Half-open lilac lisianthus flowers

Large lilac lisianthus buds

Small green lisianthus buds

Lisianthus leaves

Large green paper Mulberry leaves

When wiring floral arrangements, you will also need:

Light green floral tape

Rose wire

Wire cutters

Top tips

• Lay a piece of sponge or a soft towel over the area you are about to work on so that, if you do drop anything, it will land on something soft!

• It is better to keep arrangements fairly simple whilst you are learning the techniques to avoid breakages.

• Tape each wire individually (see below) then make small individual units of the flowers to be used, allowing a little space between the flower and leaves. Use ½-width floral tape for this and vary the sizes by adding an extra flower or bud to increase the length of the spray. Examples of these small units could be:

A rosebud and set of rose leaves taped together;

Small green buds, leaves, larger coloured buds and half-open lisianthus.

Taping a Wire

1 Cut the floral tape to ½- or ¼-width, depending on the width of stem you would like to make.

2 Stretch the tape to release the glue. Place it under the wire, positioning it just below the flower head or base of the leaf.

3 Holding the wire in one hand, squeeze the tape and the wire between your thumb and forefinger on the other hand and twist it firmly, causing the tape to stick to the wire.

4 Once the tape is attached, continue to tape down the wire for about 1.3cm (½"), keeping the tape as taut as possible, then push the tape up under the base of the flower head or leaf. By starting just below the flower head or leaf to begin with then pushing the tape up the wire, there is less chance of breaking the piece at this stage than if you were to start taping directly beneath the flower or leaf.

5 Holding the tape at an angle against the wire, continue to squeeze and twist the tape with even pressure down the length of the wire. Once the wire is covered, cut or break off any excess tape if necessary.

Top tip

Practise this technique on a length of plain wire before you attempt it on your finished piece.

Posy

A posy is a circular arrangement where the spray is assembled around the central flower or bud. A formal Victorian posy is where circlets of flowers are added around the main central flower in a formalised, geometric way by type or colour. To create other shaped arrangements, start with a posy shape and add to this to change the shape.

1 Start by holding the central flower – in this case a rose – or bud between your thumb and forefinger, just below the base of the flower head. Add a rose bud taped to its leaves and attach this underneath the rose with floral tape at the same point as your thumb and forefinger. This will be the attachment point at which the other units will be added.

2 Add a large paper mulberry leaf to the same point, underneath the rose. You now have a small, simple buttonhole/corsage arrangement: to finish it off, cut off any excess wire then tape down the stem to finish it off.

3 If you wish to continue to make a posy, add another two rose bud sprays around the central flower to form a triangular shape, attaching them at the same point that you first established under the rose.

4 Add the sprays of lisianthus and leaves around the focal flower. Gradually increase the length of the stem from the attachment point as you introduce each flower. Each new flower should reach the edge of the previous one to maintain the shape of a gentle arc.

5 Once the posy is complete, cut the excess wire from under the spray at intervals down its length to remove the bulk of wire and form a tapered effect. Finally, tape over the wire with floral tape.

6 If the spray needs to be strengthened, wind a length of rose wire around the attachment.

Teardrop/Shower

To make a small spray or shower arrangement, add a longer lisianthus spray to the front of the posy. This can be made as long as required, starting with small flowers or leaves and widening as you tape up the stem. Add this to the posy at the same attachment point as before.

Crescent/Semi-crescent

To make a crescent or semi-crescent arrangement, add the longer sprays (as above) to either side of the posy arrangement to create the shape. The difference between the two is simply that the crescent has a deeper curve than the semi-crescent.

Hogarth Curve or 'S' Shape

This is a long arrangement with a collection of flowers in the centre and trailing ends at the top and bottom, curving in opposite directions to create a gentle 'S' shape. Add a small spray of flowers or leaves at the top of the posy and curl to the left, then add a longer spray at the base of the posy and curl to the right.

'L' Shape

This arrangement has a simple 'L' shape. It is important to remember that the distribution of flowers and foliage is unequal: the height is greater than the base line. These placements of flowers and leaves should be positioned first, either straight or curved, then the central area filled out with shorter stems of flowers and foliage, but maintaining the line. Ideally they would be placed into a container or directly into a mound of pastillage and then placed on a cake, therefore eliminating the need for wiring and taping the spray together. (The other wiring techniques described here can also be formed in this way to make arrangements following their guideline shapes.)

Creativity is a great motivator because it makes people interested in what they are doing. Creativity gives hope that there can be a worthwhile idea. Creativity gives the possibility of some sort of achievement to everyone. Creativity makes life more fun and more interesting.

Edward de Bono

Elegant Expression

Longiflorum lilies are often known as Easter lilies. These beautiful white blooms have large, pendulous, trumpet-shaped flowers that bloom in the spring. They are soft, traditional yet structural and modern in appearance.

Longiflorum Lily

(Youthful innocence) Genus: Lilium

Materials

SK Pollen Style Edible Dust Food Colour: Pale Yellow

SK Professional Dust Food Colours: Edelweiss, Holly/Ivy, Leaf Green

SK Sugar Florist Paste (SFP): Pale Green, Pale Yellow, White

Equipment

Cocktail sticks

Decorative white wire

Floral tape: light green

20-, 24-, 26-, 30-gauge floral wires: white

SK Great Impressions Longiflorum Lily Veiner: medium

Trumpet former and double edge veiner tool: no. 5 (JC)

Leaf template (see page 173)

Longiflorum petal cutters (TT)

Rose wire

Basic edibles and equipment (see page 16)

Bud

1 Cut a 20-gauge floral wire in half. Make a small hook at one end with pliers.

2 Roll a ball of White SFP approximately 2.5cm (1") in diameter and form this into a cone shape, approximately 5cm (2") long.

3 Glue the hooked end of the wire and feed this up the thick end of the cone. Re-form the base of the cone around the wire with your fingers.

4 Mark three evenly spaced grooves down the length of the bud with a trumpet and double edge veiner tool.

5 Allow to semi-dry, then dust the base of the bud with a mixture of Edelweiss and Leaf Green Dust Food Colours.

Pistil

6 Cut a 24-gauge floral wire in half: you will need one piece to make a pistil (with no hook).

7 Take a small pea-sized ball of Pale Green SFP, approximately 5mm (1/8") in diameter, and form this into a small sausage shape.

8 Carefully push the wire into one end of the sausage using a drilling motion.

9 Hold the sausage of paste between your thumb and forefinger and roll it down the wire: the length of the paste should be 5cm (2"). Reshape the sausage of paste so that it is quite thin (this can also be done on a foam pad), leave the tip in a rounded shape and cut off any excess paste.

10 Make three indentations in the tip. Allow this to dry.

11 Dust the tip of the pistil with Holly/Ivy Dust Food Colour.

Stamens

12 Cut two 30-gauge wires into four pieces. Bend the end into a 'T' bar shape using pliers (see page 18).

13 Soften a very small pea-sized piece of Pale Yellow SFP; add a tiny touch of water or white vegetable fat to it if necessary.

14 Dab a little edible glue onto the wire.

15 Roll a ball of the softened SFP approximately 5mm (1/8") in diameter and form this into a tiny sausage shape. Push the glued wire into it and re-form the shape.

16 Mark a tiny line across the length of the paste with a craft knife.

17 Make six stamens in the same way and allow these to dry.

18 Lightly glue the tips of the finished stamens, then dip into Pale Yellow Pollen Dust and allow to dry.

19 Dust the wires with a mixture of Leaf Green and Edelweiss Dust Food Colours.

20 Cut some light green floral tape into three equal lengths. Position three stamens just below the pistil tip and tape them to the wire. Add the other three stamens to form a circle around the pistil (again, just below it) and tape again.

Petals

21 Roll out some White SFP on a greased rolling board and cut out the petals with the Longiflorum lily cutters. You will need to make three inner (wider) petals and three outer (narrower) petals.

22 Insert a 26-gauge wire into each petal using your preferred method of wiring (see pages 19 to 22).

23 Vein each petal with the veiner, place on a foam pad and enhance the

central vein with the double edge veiner tool.

24 Soften but do not frill the edges of the petal with a ball tool. Use a cocktail stick to gently curl the petal inwards from the tip. Hold the petal between your thumb and forefinger and curve it back slightly.

25 Make all six petals in the same way. Allow them to set off (hold their shape) but not dry completely.

26 Mix some Edelweiss and Leaf Green Dust Colours together to make soft green. Dust the base of each petal on either side using a dry, flat dusting brush.

Flower Assembly

27 Assemble the petals while they are still semi-dry. Using ½-width light green floral tape, firmly tape each large petal individually around the base of the prepared pistil and stamens. Next, tape the narrow outer petals in the space behind and between the large ones, again firmly and individually.

28 Cut a 20-gauge floral wire into three pieces. At this point you may require a stronger stem, so add a 20-gauge wire at the base of the flower. Tape down the length of the wire with ½-width floral tape.

29 If the flower will not hold its shape, form some kitchen foil into a cone, dust with cornflour and place the flower into this until it hardens in the required shape.

Leaves

30 Cut a 26-gauge wire into three lengths.

31 Roll out some Pale Green SFP. Cut out the leaf shape using the template and wire using your preferred method (see pages 19 to 22).

32 Place the leaf onto a foam pad and soften the edge with a ball tool.

33 Mark veins on the leaf using the pointed end of a Dresden tool. Gently curve the leaf back slightly. Make further leaves in the same way.

34 Dust the leaves with Leaf Green Dust Food Colour then pass through steam to set the colour.

Spray Assembly

35 Cut a small piece of ½-width light green floral tape. Tape two or three leaves around each of the buds, then tape one or two leaves below the flowers. These component parts are now ready for the arrangement.

36 If you are making the candleholder arrangement, start with a bud and leaves and tape a flower and leaves below it. Line this up against the candleholder and attach them to it using a 20cm (8") length of rose wire twisted around the candleholder and flower stem. Pull the wire tight to secure them in place. The wire can be threaded through the flower or leaf to make them more secure but take extra care when doing this.

37 Take the next flower, bud and leaves taped together and attach them as above. Repeat again with the other flowers until you have the desired effect.

38 Cover the wire with floral tape to tidy and hide the wires in the arrangement.

For the Arrangement

6 Longiflorum lilies, 1 half (semi-open) flower, 3 buds

13 leaves

Tall candleholder

Decorative wire: white

For a simple, elegant display the flowers have been arranged around a tall, black candlestick which makes a lovely keepsake. The display is finished off with a simple twist of white decorative wire. This could stand beside a cake decorated with perhaps just a single lily bloom.

What we have to learn to do, we learn by doing.

Aristotle

Simple Splendour

This beautiful poppy is a tall and majestic plant; its large, white flowers have petals that look like wrinkled crêpe paper. They have large, yellow, ball-like centres and blue-green foliage. I like to think of it as the queen of all flowers.

Matilija Poppy

(Consolation) Genus: Romneya

Materials

SK Pollen Style Edible Dust Colour: Pale Golden

SK Professional Dust Food Colours: Bluegrass, Cyclamen, Edelweiss, Holly/Ivy

SK Sugar Florist Paste (SFP): Pale Green, White

Equipment

Fine cotton thread: yellow (Gutermann colour 106)

Floral tape: light green

20-, 26- 28-, 30-gauge floral wires: white

Petal and calyx templates (see page 173)

Petal veiner: no. 18 (CC)

Polystrene formers/apple tray

Texturing/frilling tool: no. 12 (JC)

Basic edibles and equipment (see page 16)

Centre

1 Cut a 30-gauge floral wire in half.

2 Wind some fine, yellow cotton thread around two fingers, spread open about 4cm (1½"), approximately 80 times.

3 Remove the cotton from your fingers then fold and twist it into a figure of '8'. Fold this in half to make a smaller loop.

4 Cut a 28-gauge floral wire into two equal lengths. Thread a piece of wire through the cotton loop then fold it in half over the cotton. Twist the wire tightly around the cotton (this will support the ovary). Ensure the cotton is positioned just below this and continue to twist the rest of the wire below the cotton to secure it tightly in place.

5 Cut through the top of the cotton loop and separate the strands, creating the stamens. Spread the cotton and trim the ends of the strands into a fan shape.

6 Open the cotton to expose the central wire. Dust just the centre around the wire with Cyclamen Dust Food Colour.

7 To make the seedpod, form a pea-sized piece of Pale Green SFP into a cone shape. Grease a glass-headed pin or piece of wire with white vegetable fat and insert this into the pointed end of the cone to make it easier to hold. Flatten the top of the cone and use small tweezers to pinch six tiny ridges onto the flat part. Leave this to dry slightly.

8 Glue the wire in the centre of the cotton and push the seedpod onto the wire. Leave to dry.

9 Brush a small amount of edible glue around the seedpod and stick a few cotton stamens to it. Flatten the cotton stamens together, glue the tips, then dip the ends into Pale Golden Pollen Dust.

Petals

10 Cut two 26-gauge white wires each into three equal lengths.

11 Roll out some White SFP and cut out the petals using the template. Wire each petal using your preferred method (see pages 19 to 22).

12 Dust the petal veiner with cornflour and place a petal between the two halves to create a deeply frilled petal. Use the texturing tool on the edges of the petal to increase the frilling.

13 Place each petal in an apple tray cup or former and allow to semi-dry in a gently curved shape. Once the petals are almost dry they are ready to assemble: the petals will hold their shape as you move them but will be flexible enough to reshape slightly once in position if necessary.

14 Repeat this process to make six petals.

Assembling the Flower

15   Using ½-width light green floral tape, tape three inner petals around the prepared centre one at a time. Ensure they are all held in place tightly.

16   Repeat the process with the outer petals: position these over the gaps between the other petals and ensure that no two petals are directly behind each other.

17   Cut a 20-gauge wire in half. Tape a piece of wire directly under the flower head to strengthen the stem, then continue taping down the length of the wire.

Buds

18   Cut a 20-gauge white floral wire in half and make a hook in one end of each length.

19   Form a ball of White SFP approximately 4cm (1½") in diameter.

20   Lightly glue the hooked wire, insert it into the ball of paste and re-form the base. Allow this to dry.

21   Roll out some White SFP and cut out two bud petals using the template. Frill each petal with a texturing tool.

22   Brush some edible glue onto the dried bud shape and place the petals onto it so that they are opposite each other. Re-form the base.

23   Cut out two calyx shapes from Pale Green SFP, brush each one with edible glue and stick them to the tip of the bud on either side.

24   Turn the bud over and use fine scissors to make tiny cuts into the paste all over the calyx to texture the surface. Dust the calyx with Holly/Ivy mixed with Edelweiss and a tiny amount of Bluegrass Dust Food Colour.

25   Repeat to make another two buds in the same way.

Leaves

26   The leaves are made from light green floral tape. Cut pieces of tape into 4cm (1½") lengths, then cut them into long, narrow leaf shapes. Cut tiny 'V' shapes into the edges and attach the leaves underneath the buds.

Top tip   Use very fine, pointed scissors to cut the calyx shapes and bud, keeping the cuts close to each other for a more realistic effect.

For the Cakes

10cm, 15cm and 20cm (4", 6" and 8") tall round cakes, placed on cake boards and covered with white sugarpaste (see pages 168 to 172)

SK CMC gum

Varipin (JC)

7 poppies

3 buds

3 posy picks

3 lengths of floral reeds or decorative wire

Glass cake stands

SK Sugar Florist Paste (SFP): White

Butterfly paper punch

SK Magic Sparkles Metallic Dust Food Colour

After the cakes have been covered, roll out a 5cm (2") border of leftover sugarpaste mixed with a small amount of CMC gum. Roll over the paste again with a Varipin to texture the surface. Cut out a length of the paste to fit around each cake and attach around the base with edible glue.

Tape together three groups of flowers with buds and insert them into posy picks then into the cake tops. To link the three cakes together, place them on glass stands and then make an arc from reeds or decorative wire. Insert the ends into a posy pick in the same way as for the flowers.

For extra decoration, thinly roll out some White SFP and allow to semi-dry. Cut out several butterflies using a paper punch. Brush them with Magic Sparkles Metallic Dust and allow to dry with the wings slightly lifted. Attach to the cakes with a little edible glue or royal icing.

Persistence is its own reward.

(A saying)

Shades of Spring

The primrose is native to Britain and continental Europe and is extremely popular in gardens. It is a small plant, typically no more than 10cm (4") high, which produces pretty cream to yellow flowers; other colours are also found in the species.

Primrose

(Young love) Genus: Primula

Materials

SK CMC gum

SK Sugar Florist Paste (SFP): Pale Green, Pale Yellow, White

SK Professional Liquid Food Colour: Marigold

SK Professional Paste Food Colours: Daffodil, Leaf Green, Sunflower

SK Professional Dust Food Colours: Daffodil, Holly/Ivy, Marigold. Vine

Equipment

Apple trays

Five petal veining tool: no. 7 (JC)

Floral tape: light green

26-gauge floral wire: light green

SK Great Impressions Primrose Veiner: medium

Kitchen roll

Leaf template (see page 173)

Petal veiner/friller tool: no. 12 (JC)

Primrose cutter (FMM)

Small calyx (jasmine) cutter (FMM)

Varipin (JC)

Basic edibles and equipment (see page 16)

Flowers

1 Cut a 26-gauge light green floral wire into three equal lengths and make a hook at one end.

2 Roll a pea-sized piece of Pale Yellow SFP and form this into a cone. If a paler flower is required, mix some White SFP into the Pale Yellow. Place this onto a greased area of a non-stick board and make a Mexican hat shape (see pages 16 to 17).

3 Lift the paste and place it on an area of the board which has not been greased. Place the cutter over the hat shape, press firmly then remove the cutter.

4 Place the flower into a hole in the foam pad. Gently soften each petal with a ball tool, then texture the petals with the five-petal veining tool.

5 Press into the centre of the flower with the five-pointed end of the veining tool: line up the tool with the centre of the heart shaped petals. This creates a star shape.

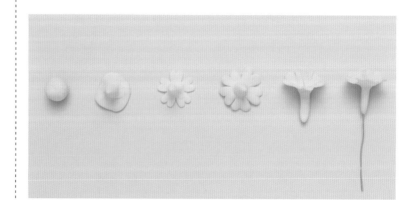

6 Glue the hooked end of the wire and push it into the centre of the flower. Leave a tiny amount of the wire hook showing to resemble a single stamen in the centre of the flower. Reshape the base.

Calyx

7 Make another Mexican hat shape using a pea-sized ball of Pale Green SFP. Cut out the calyx with a tiny calyx cutter, keeping the bump in the middle.

8 Remove the calyx from the board, dust the base with cornflour and push the pointed end of a CelStick into the centre. Gently push the paste against the stick to hold it in place.

9 Using tweezers, pinch a ridge in the centre of each individual point from the tip to the base.

10 Carefully remove the calyx from the CelStick; take care not to hold it too tightly otherwise you will distort the shape.

11 Brush a small amount of edible glue onto the base of the flower. Thread the wired flower through the centre of the calyx then push the calyx up the wire and onto the base of the flower. It should sit underneath the base of the petals. Allow to dry.

12 Cut some pale green floral tape to 1/3 width and tape down the stem.

Leaves

13 To make the leaf colour, add some Leaf Green and a touch of Daffodil Paste Food Colours to some Pale Green SFP.

14 Cut a 26-gauge wire into three equal pieces.

15 Make the leaves using the template and your preferred method for wiring (see pages 19 to 22). Vein the leaves with a primrose veiner and gently soften the edges with a ball tool.

16 Give the leaves some movement by drying them in curved shapes on crumpled kitchen roll.

Dusting and Colouring

17 Use Marigold Liquid Food Colour and a no. 0 paintbrush to carefully paint the star shape in the centre of the flowers.

18 Dust the leaves with Leaf Green, then brush Holly/Ivy mixed with Leaf Green down the centre. Steam the leaves to set the colour.

19 Dust the flowers with a small amount of Daffodil Dust Food Colour, steam and allow to dry.

Assembly

20 Tape the flowers and buds together at the base to form a cluster and then tape the leaves from the base around them.

Camellias are evergreen shrubs with glossy leaves; their flowers are usually large and conspicuous with five to nine petals. They are grown as ornamental plants and their colours vary from white through pink to red.

Camellia

(Graciousness) Species: Camellia reticulata

Materials

SK Confectioners' Glaze

SK Professional Dust Food Colours: Cyclamen, Daffodil, Edelweiss, Vine

SK Professional Paste Food Colours: Holly/Ivy, Leaf Green

SK Sugar Florist Paste (SFP): Pale Green, Pale Pink

Equipment

Apple trays

Cornhusk veiner

22-, 26-gauge floral wires: green

24-gauge floral wires: white

SK Glaze Cleaner (IPA)

SK Great Impressions Camellia Leaf Veiner: medium

Large rose petals cutters: 6cm, 4cm (TT)

Leaf template (see page 173)

Small seed head stamens: white

Basic edibles and equipment (see page 16)

Centre

1 To form the pistil, cut a piece of light green floral tape approximately 6cm (2½") in length, then cut to ⅓ width, leaving some of the tape uncut at the end. Twist the three cut pieces into fine strands.

2 Cut a 24-gauge floral wire into three pieces. Tape the untwisted tape to a wire then bend the top of the wire down over the tape to hold it in position. Continue taping down the wire to neaten it.

3 Take half a bunch of seed head stamens and divide them into small bunches. Glue the middle of each bunch with PVA glue, allow these to dry and then cut them in half. Glue the base of each cut bunch and stick them around the prepared centre. Allow the glue to dry.

4 Dust the stamens with Daffodil Dust Food Colour. Cut the pistil strands level with the stamens. When dry, gently pull the stamens away from the centre using tweezers.

Buds

5   Cut a 22-gauge wire into three. Make a small hook at one end.

6   Form a small ball of Pale Pink SFP. Glue the hooked wire, push this into the ball of paste and reshape it.

7   Make five indentations on the top of the ball of paste with a cutting wheel, then dust the bud with a mixture of Cyclamen and Edelweiss Dust Food Colours.

8   Mix some Pale Green SFP with Leaf Green Paste Food Colour to make a brighter green. Roll out the paste and cut out four small petal shapes for the sepals (these are easy to do freehand). Soften the edges with a ball tool.

9   Glue the base of one sepal and attach it to the base of the bud. Repeat this with the other sepals around the bud.

Top tip   If you would like to make the stamens a richer colour, add some Sunflower Dust Food Colour to the Daffodil.

Petals

10   Soften some Pale Pink SFP by kneading in a little white vegetable fat.

11   Cut a 26-gauge wire cut to three equal lengths and use one piece for each petal. Use the largest and second largest rose petal cutters to make five wired petals in each size following your preferred method for wiring (see pages 19 to 22).

12   Once you have cut out each petal, cut into the tip of the petal using the pointed end of the cutter to form a heart shape.

13   Press a ball tool into the pointed cut areas in a circular motion to soften the sharp points.

14   Vein the petal with a cornhusk and then gently soften the edges with a ball tool. Place into a food-grade polythene bag while you are making the others.

15   Allow the petals to semi-dry with a slight curve in an apple tray.

16 Using a mixture of Cyclamen and Edelweiss Dust Food Colours, dust the base of each petal on the front and the back then catch the edges of the petals with the dust. Steam the petals to set the colour.

Assembling the Flower

17 To assemble the flower, cut some light green tape to ½-width. Tape the smaller petals around the prepared centre, then the larger ones behind and in between the spaces of the first ones. If you need to strengthen the stem, add a 22-gauge wire before taping down the length of the stem.

Leaves

18 Add some Holly/Ivy Paste Food Colour to some Holly/Ivy SFP to darken it.

19 Use the leaf template and 26-gauge wires to make the leaves following your chosen method (see pages 19 to 22).

20 Vein each leaf with a camellia leaf veiner.

21 Place each leaf onto a non-stick board and serrate the edges with a Dresden tool, just nipping into the sugar at an angle up each side of the leaf.

22 Soften the edges with a ball tool then allow to semi-dry on a curved former (such as an apple tray).

23 Dust the semi-dry leaves with Vine green, using a little on the top of the leaf and more on the base.

24 Steam the leaves to set the colour and then dip into ¼-strength confectioners' glaze (a mixture of ¼ glaze and ¾ glaze cleaner).

Top tip

To give leaves more of a shine, make the glaze solution stronger (i.e. use a higher proportion of glaze to glaze cleaner).

Daffodils are the flower of friendship and belong to the genus Narcissus. Dating back over many centuries they are constantly recurring flowers which flourish in clusters in the spring and brighten the countryside with their show of cream to bright yellow blooms.

Daffodil

(Chivalry) Genus: Narcissus

Materials

SK Sugar Florist Paste (SFP): Daffodil
SK Professional Dust Food Colours:
Berberis, Bluebell, Daffodil, Edelweiss,
Holly/Ivy, Leaf Green, Sunflower
SK Pollen Style Edible Dust Colour: Pale
Golden

Equipment

Cocktail sticks

Cornhusk or veiner

Floral tape: beige, green

20-, 22-, 24-gauge floral wires: white

26-gauge floral wires: white (for the
botanical method)

Long, sharp scissors

Petal veiner/friller tool: no. 12 (JC)

Seed head stamens: white

Six-petal flower cutter: no. N1 (OP)

**Basic edibles and equipment (see
page 16)**

Centre

1 To make the daffodil centre using a simple method, take six white seed head stamens and fold them in half. Position a single stamen above the others to represent the pistil.

2 Using a small amount of PVA glue, glue three stamens together at the base and then repeat this with the other three stamens. Place the pistil onto this so that it protrudes just above the stamen heads and glue to the stamens.

3 Cut a 20-gauge floral wire in half (do not make a hook this time). Glue both bunches of stamens to a length of wire, slightly above the end. Leave to dry.

4 Cut a small length of floral tape in half and tape 1cm (³⁄₈") down from the stamen heads to neaten them. It is not necessary to tape down the length of the wire.

5 Dip the prepared stamens/pistil into Pale Golden Pollen Dust Colour.

Top tip

If you would like to make a more botanically correct centre, form a tiny bud of paste on the end of a 26-gauge wire, roll the paste down the wire approximately 1cm ($^3/_8$") and divide the top into three sections. This forms the pistil.

Roll and form a tiny piece of Daffodil SFP into a long, very thin sausage and cut this into six thin pieces. Allow to semi-dry then attach the pieces around and under the pistil head with edible glue.

Trumpet (Corolla)

6 Roll a small ball of Daffodil SFP, approximately 1cm ($^3/_8$") in diameter. Form the ball into a cone shape.

7 Put some white vegetable fat onto the tip of a CelStick and push this into the wide end of the cone. Soften and thin the open end of the paste around the CelStick and remove it.

8 Check that the cone has not elongated too much; if so cut some of some paste off at the base and reshape it. Use a friller tool or a cocktail stick to frill around the edges of the open end.

9 Place the trumpet onto a cornhusk with the lines horizontal. Use the friller tool to frill and vein both the inside and outside of the trumpet.

10 Push the prepared centre into the trumpet and reshape this around the base again. The stamens and pistil should be within the trumpet and not protruding out of it.

Petals

11 Roll a ball of Daffodil SFP approximately 1.5cm ($^5/_8$") in diameter, then form this into a cone. Make this into a Mexican hat shape (see pages 16 to 17) then cut out a flower shape using a six-petal flower cutter.

12 Place the flower onto a foam pad and widen each petal individually with the ball tool. Vein each petal individually with the cornhusk.

13 Place the flower back onto the foam pad, mark a central vein down each petal and then pinch the tips.

14 Open up the centre of the flower with the pointed end of the CelStick and brush edible glue in the opening. Push the prepared trumpet into the centre and carefully pull down until it rests on the petals.

15 Hang the flower upside down until it starts to set off, then open it into the desired position, either half open or fully open. Gently coax and lift alternate petals inwards, leaving the other three to sit behind and in between these.

16 Mark a tiny hip, i.e. an oval shape 5mm (1/8") long, at the base of the flower. Press into and around the paste with a palette knife to represent the seedpod.

17 It may be necessary to strengthen the flower stem if it is going to stand in the arrangement, in which case add a 22-gauge wire underneath the flower head and tape down the length with light green floral tape.

Buds

18 Roll a small piece of Daffodil SFP into a ball measuring 2cm (¾"), then form into a cone.

19 Cut a 22-gauge wire in half, make a hook in the end of one piece and push it into the pointed end of the cone.

20 Form the wide end into a point and mark five indentations from the tip to the base using a cutting wheel. Allow this to dry.

Colouring

21 Dust the base of the bud with Leaf Green Dust Food Colour.

22 Dust the hip of the flower with Leaf Green Dust. Dust up the base with Leaf Green mixed with a small amount of Edelweiss Dust to keep it pale.

23 Dust the flower petals and trumpet with Daffodil and Sunflower to obtain some variation of colour. Catch the edges of some of the flower trumpets with Sunflower mixed with Berberis.

Spathe

24 To make the spathe that sits around the ovary and buds, cut a small length of beige floral tape to approximately 5cm (2") and cut the tip into a point. Stretch the tape, place it onto a foam pad and mark lines on it with a Dresden tool.

25 Attach a spathe to the base of both the flowers and buds. Using a pair of pliers, bend the heads of the flowers at right angles to the stems.

Leaves

The leaves can be made with either paste or floral tape; I have chosen to use tape here but you can follow one of the methods described on pages 19 to 22 if you prefer to make the leaves from paste.

26 Cut a length of tape, stretch it and place it onto the board. Glue half of the tape with PVA glue then place a 24-gauge floral wire halfway along the tape and fold it over, leaving an area without wire. Press firmly to stick the tape in place then leave this to dry completely.

27 Using a pair of long, sharp scissors, cut down the leaf from the tip down either side of the wire to shape it and then cut the tip into a point.

28 Dust the leaf with a mixture of Holly/Ivy, Bluebell and Edelweiss Dust Food Colours (daffodil leaves have a slight blue tinge to them). Steam the leaves and the daffodil flowers to set the colour.

29 Daffodil leaves grow from ground level besides the flower and not on the stems, so place them near the flowers rather than taping them together.

Catkins form on the trees in the summer months but remain tight and closed all winter. They begin to expand in early spring, often before the leaves appear or get too large. There are many species of trees that bear elegant hanging catkins.

Hazel Catkins

Genus: *Corylus avellana*

Materials

SK Sugar Florist Paste (SFP): Pale Green, Pale Yellow
SK Pollen Style Edible Dust Colour: Pale Golden

Equipment

Cotton thread: white
20-gauge floral wire: white
Floral tape: brown

Basic edibles and equipment (see page 16)

Sprouting Branches

1 Make a hook in the end of a 20-gauge wire. Hold the wire with one hand and with pointed pliers, make a small bend in it approximately 6cm (2³/₈") down from the top. Squeeze the bend tightly together and straighten the wire below. Repeat the process to make three or four bends in the wire, positioned alternately down the length.

2 Make approximately five of these wires altogether: they will form the branches for the catkins to hang from.

Catkins

Because the catkins are on threads they will swing gently on the branches, making them look realistic.

3 Cut several pieces of thread approximately 15cm (6") long.

4 Roll a pea-sized piece of Pale Yellow SFP, form this into a sausage shape and flatten it.

5 Brush a thin line of edible glue down the centre of the paste and place the cotton over this. Fold the paste in half. Roll the paste into a sausage shape approximately 4cm (1½") long.

6 Cut tiny 'V' shapes down and around the length of paste from the cotton to the tip. Allow to dry.

7 Brush edible glue over the entire length of paste and roll in Pale Golden Pollen Dust. Allow to dry again.

8 Dust the catkin with Sunflower Dust Food Colour then paint tiny lines of Leaf Green Dust Colour mixed with clear alcohol in fine stripes around the catkin.

9 Repeat to make as many catkins as required and allow to dry.

10 Group the catkins together in twos and threes and wrap the cotton around the wire where the notches are. Leave some notches free for the buds. If there is excess cotton, leave it as it can be taped to the wire later.

11 Repeat the step above to make approximately five branches with catkins.

12 Cut a length of brown floral tape in half and tape down the wire. At the catkins' hanging point, tape any excess thread to the wire.

13 Tape down further, add in another branch with catkins and continue down the branch. Repeat the process with the other branches.

14 For the buds, form tiny balls of Pale Green SFP, brush the notches with edible glue and stick the buds over these. Reshape each bud into a point.

Top tip Catkins can be used in any spring arrangement to add space and movement to the display.

For the Cake

Fruit cake for 23cm (9") oval cake, baked in two batches in a rugby ball tin (W)

1.5kg (3lb 5oz) marzipan (SK)

2kg (4lb 6½ oz) sugarpaste: white

15cm (6") oval cake drum

15cm (6") oval thin cake board

250g pack Instant Mix Pastillage (SK)

2 branches of catkins

8 daffodils

5 daffodil buds

8 daffodil leaves

9 primroses

3 primrose buds

9 primrose leaves

3 camellias

Level the cakes and sandwich them together (see pages 168 to 171). Place the cake on the oval cake drum, brush the cake with boiled apricot jam and fill in the join if required with a sausage of marzipan. Cover the cake with marzipan, taking care to maintain the shape, and leave to firm for 24 hours.

Cover the cake with sugarpaste (see pages 168 to 172), again maintaining the shape, and allow to firm for several hours.

Make some very firm pastillage by using less water than recommended on the

pack. Form the paste into a dome shape and stick it onto the thin oval card. This will be the base for the flowers to be arranged in. Stick the board onto the cake.

Start the arrangement by pushing the catkins into the pastillage. Position them at the back to create height (they need to be approximately twice or two-and-a-half times the height of the cake).

Next, arrange the daffodils and leaves in front of and around the catkins.

Stick some camellia leaves around the base to cover the pastillage then place the primroses at the side. Finally add two camellia flowers in the centre at different heights. You could make an extra camellia flower and place this at the base of the arrangement for added effect.

The little that is completed, vanishes from the sight of one who looks forward to what is still to do.

Johann Wolfgang von Goethe

Cascading Fuchsias

The fuchsia originated in the Caribbean, where it was growing wild. It was first imported into Britain around 1789, and the flowers were highly valued by the Victorians. There are over 100 species of fuchsias and they come in a kaleidoscope of wonderfully vibrant colours.

Fuchsia

(Good taste) Family: Onagraceae

Materials

SK Professional Dust Food Colours: Fuchsia, Leaf Green

SK Professional Paste Food Colours: Fuchsia, Leaf Green

SK Sugar Florist Paste (SFP): Pale Green, White

Equipment

22-, 24-, 26-, 28-gauge floral wires: green

Fuchsia sepal cutter (from set of 2): 6cm (TT)

SK Great Impressions Tea Rose Leaf Veiner: large/6cm

Rose leaf cutters: set of 3 (FMM)

Rose petal cutters: 3cm, 2.8cm (TT)

Small, matt, round seed head stamens

Very fine paintbrush: no. 0000

Basic edibles and equipment (see page 16)

Centre

1 Cut a 24-gauge green floral wire into thirds.

2 Take nine round-headed stamens and cut off each tip at one end. Arrange them at different lengths, leaving one longer than the rest to form the pistil.

3 Glue the cut end of the stamens around a piece of 24-gauge wire. Leave this to dry.

4 Form a very tiny piece of White SFP into a ball. Brush some edible glue onto the base of the stamens and wire, stick the ball of paste over this and re-form the ball shape. Leave to dry.

5 Mix some Fuchsia Dust Food Colour with either clear alcohol or rosewater to create an edible paint. Use this to paint the stamens and allow to dry.

Top tip The stamens of fuchsias are usually the same colour as the sepals.

Petals/Skirt

6 Grease an area of a non-stick board with white vegetable fat. Thinly roll out some White SFP on the greased area and cut out four petals with the 3cm rose petal cutter.

7 Work on one petal at a time, keeping the others covered under a sheet of cling film or polythene. Gently texture the wide end of the petal with the texturing tool. Soften the edge and frill the base with a ball tool, then gently cup the centre.

8 Using the fuchsia-coloured paint made earlier, paint fine lines from the pointed end to halfway up the petal.

9 Repeat the process with the other three petals.

10 Glue the base of a petal a little way up one side. Stick it to the tiny ball of flower paste on the prepared stamens. Repeat this with the other three petals, overlapping the previous one each time. If you prefer, you can glue and overlap the petals on the board and then all four petals can be attached at once. Place into a former or hang upside down to dry.

11 For the double fuchsia, make a further four petals in the same way using the smaller cutter. These petals will form the inner set. Attach the four larger outer petals one at a time to the outside of the inner set, placing each one in between the petals of the previous four.

12 To prevent the petals from drying completely, place them into a polythene food-grade bag but leave the end open whilst the others are being made.

Sepals

13 Mix some Fuchsia Paste Food Colour into a ball of the White SFP to make a full-strength fuchsia colour.

14 Form a small ball of paste into a cone, pinch out the edges then form into a Mexican hat shape (see pages 16 to 17). Place the fuchsia sepal cutter over this and cut out the shape.

15 Turn over the paste and push the end of a CelStick into the centre to open it and widen the hole. Roll the paste through your fingers, working up the pedicel (stem) to thin it. Cut off any excess paste and re-form.

16 Place the flower shape onto the foam pad and use the ball tool to press gently from the tip of each point to the centre, curling each sepal upwards. Allow to semi-dry.

Flowers

17   Glue the centre of the sepals and push the wired petals through the centre, including the pedicel, so that the sepals sit away from the petals. Allow to dry upright until the sepals hold their shape.

18   Make a very tiny ball of Pale Green SFP and form into an oval. Open up the centre with a cocktail stick and apply some edible glue. Feed the wire through this and push the oval down onto the pedicel to form the tiny seedpod.

Top tip

It is a good idea to make extra flowers to allow for breakages.

Buds

19   Make the buds using either Pale Green or fuchsia coloured SFP; the green buds should be smaller than the fuchsia coloured buds. Form a ball of paste into a pear shape with a point at the wide end.

20   Cut a 28-gauge green floral wire into four and make a tiny hook at one end. Glue the hook and feed the wire into the thin end of the paste, then roll the paste up the wire in the same way as for the sepals. Form a very tiny ball to make a seedpod.

21   Divide the bud at the pointed end into three and cut into the paste with a cutting wheel to make the divisions. Dust with Leaf Green and Fuchsia Dust Food Colours.

Leaves

22   Cut a 28-gauge wire into three equal lengths.

23   Make the leaves using Pale Green SFP mixed with Leaf Green Paste Food Colour. Use your chosen method to wire the leaves (see pages 19 to 22) and cut out each one with

a rose leaf cutter. Vein it with the rose leaf veiner. Repeat the process to make several leaves in each size. Soften the edges with a ball tool to create movement.

24 Allow the leaves to semi-dry then dust with Leaf Green Dust Food Colour. Brush a little Fuchsia onto the edges.

25 Use a very fine paintbrush (no. 0000) and either Fuchsia Liquid Food Colour or Fuchsia Dust mixed with clear alcohol to paint lightly over the main veins in the leaves.

26 Steam the finished leaves and allow to dry again.

Assembly

27 Tape two or three small, green buds onto a 22-gauge wire using ½-width light green floral tape. Leave approximately 2.5cm (1") of wire showing on the buds so that they hang down slightly. Dust with Leaf Green if necessary.

28 Add a two or three small leaves above the buds, again leaving some wire showing.

29 Continue taping along the wire, adding a flower and some buds. Tape in some more leaves in varying sizes above these. Continue down the wire, adding a flower or two at the same point, then add the leaves above.

Top tip The flowers grow in clusters on the plant but in sugar they are very vulnerable to breakage so should be spaced a little further apart. Take extra care when transporting fuchsias made in sugar.

For the Arrangement

Decorative wire: fuchsia pink

9 fuchsia flowers

3 fuchsia coloured buds

10 green buds, various sizes

Approximately 45-50 leaves (15-18 for each stem)

Vase with narrow neck

In the arrangement shown I have made three stems of flowers and foliage and placed them into a vase. To complement the colour of the flowers I have added some decorative wire.

If you wish to use this arrangement on a cake, push the wires into a posy pick before inserting this into the cake. Use tweezers or pliers to handle the flowers.

Go as far as you can see; when you get there you'll be able to see further.

Thomas Carlyle

Autumnal Tones

Montbretia have splendid spikes of orange/red, tubular, trumpet-shaped flowers that are held above the foliage on long stems and sit amid sword-like foliage. These tall, elegant flowers add height to an arrangement and are surprisingly easy to make.

Montbretia
Genus: Crocosmia

Materials

SK Sugar Florist Paste (SFP): Marigold, Pale Green, Pale Yellow

SK Professional Dust Food Colours: Holly/Ivy, Leaf Green, Poinsettia, Sunflower

Equipment

22-, 28-, 33-gauge floral wires: green

Leaf template (see page 173)

Six-petal flower cutter: no. N5 (OP)

Very fine, round head stamens

Basic edibles and equipment (see page 16)

Buds

1 Cut three or four lengths of 33-gauge wire into four equal pieces and make a tiny hook at one end of each.

2 Mix some Marigold Paste Food Colour into a small piece of Pale Yellow SFP to brighten the colour.

3 Form a tiny ball of the prepared yellow paste, approximately 5mm (1/8") in diameter. Brush a little edible glue onto the hook of a wire and push the paste onto it. Form into a tiny pear shape. Using fine scissors, cut tiny 'v' shapes at the base opposite each other to represent the calyx.

4 Repeat the process to make approximately 15 buds, gradually increasing the size to approximately 2cm (¾"). For the larger buds, taper the paste down the wire to slim and elongate it then cut the calyx at the base as before. Divide the tips of

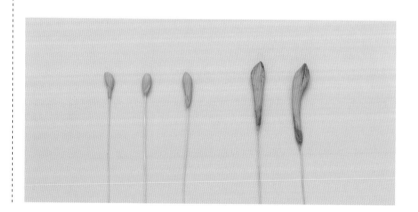

the larger buds into three with a craft knife then re-shape them into a soft point.

5 To make a half-open flower, make a larger bud and push a cocktail stick into the top to open it, then push the tip of a CelStick into the hole to widen and thin it. Make three cuts into the opening with fine scissors, then snip off the squared edges and soften these with your fingers.

6 To dust the buds, brush Poinsettia Dust Food Colour on their tips and Leaf Green on the calyx.

Pistil and Stamens

7 To make the pistil, cut the heads off both ends of three fine stamens. Glue down the length of the stamens, leaving the tips unglued, and stick them together.

8 Take three fine stamens and cut off the heads at one end. Using PVA glue, glue the base of the stamens around the pistil, so the stamen heads are just below it. Leave to dry.

Flower Heads

9 Cut a 28-gauge wire into three equal lengths and make a tiny hook at one end of each piece.

10 Form a small ball of the yellow coloured SFP into a cone shape and flatten the base. Place it onto the board and roll out the base thinly to make a slim Mexican hat shape approximately 12mm (½") wide (see pages 16 to 17).

11 Place the six-petal flower cutter over the top, cut out the shape then remove the cutter. Turn the flower over and use the point of a CelStick to open up the centre of the flower.

12 Glue the hooked end of a wire and push the wire into the opening, then pull it down through the flower until the hook is embedded in the paste.

13 Measure and cut the prepared stamens so they just protrude from the flower. Brush a tiny amount of edible glue at the base and push them into

the centre of the flower using tweezers. Re-form the paste underneath the flower head if required.

14 Dust the base of the flower with Leaf Green then brush some Sunflower into the centre to colour the flower and the stamens. Dust the tips of the petals with Poinsettia Dust Food Colour.

15 Allow the flowers to dry.

Assembly

16 Cut some light green floral paste into three along the length to make $1/3$-width tape.

17 Starting with the smallest bud, tape the wire around it. Add another bud and bend the wire below it to create a zig-zag effect. Add more small buds individually below the bend and on alternate sides to keep the zig-zag shape all the way down the stem. The smallest buds should be quite close together with the space between them increasing as they get larger down the stem. Finally, add the flowers at the bottom of the stem.

18 Repeat to make further stems at different lengths (you will need three for this arrangement).

Leaves

19 The leaves are long and therefore need more support, so you will need to use 22-gauge wires. Make these following your chosen method (see pages 19 to 22) and use the template and cutting wheel to cut them out.

20 Place each leaf onto a soft foam pad and score the surface gently from the top to the bottom with a scriber to make the veining on the back and front of the leaf.

21 Soften the edges with a ball tool but do not frill them. Allow to dry.

22 Dust the leaves with Leaf Green Dust Food Colour and pass through steam to set the colour. Allow to dry before using in an arrangement.

The Helleborus genus is native to much of Europe. Its species are used widely for decorative purposes and are particularly valued by gardeners for their winter and early spring flowering. The colours range from white and yellow to greenish purple and pinks to near black.

Hellebore

(Scandal) Species: Orientalis

Materials

SK Confectioners' Glaze

SK Dust Food Colours: Cyclamen, Holly/Ivy, Leaf Green, Sunflower

SK Sugar Florist Paste (SFP): Cream, Pale Green

Equipment

Cornhusk or veiner

Fine, round seed head stamens

28-gauge floral wires: green

26-gauge floral wires: white

SK Glaze Cleaner (IPA)

SK Great Impressions Orientalis Hellebore Leaf Veiner

Leaf templates (see page 173)

4cm rose petal cutter (TT)

Six-petal flower cutter: no. N5 (OP)

Small toothbrush (new) or stiff paintbrush

Basic edibles and equipment (see page 16)

Pistil

1 Cut a 6.5cm (2½") length of pale green floral tape. Stretch the tape and cut it lengthwise into ¼-width pieces. Twist each one into a very thin strand then cut off pieces approximately 5cm (2") long. Make five per flower.

2 Cut a 26-gauge green wire into three equal lengths. Take five fine strands of twisted floral tape and line a wire up just above the base of the fine twisted tape pieces. Use a piece of ¼-width floral tape to attach the strands to the wire, then fold the wire over the tape and tape over it again. This prevents the wire from being pulled out.

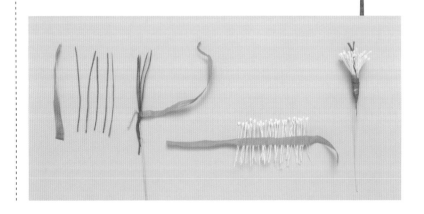

Stamens

3 Cut a bunch of seed head stamens in half (the stamens are numerous in this flower).

4 Cut a 13cm (5") length of pale green floral tape and cut this into three lengthways. Stretch the tape then brush PVA glue over each length. Place the stamens over this so the tips are 1.5cm (½") above the tape. Allow this to dry.

5 Take the prepared pistil and wrap the stamens around it. Tape over the base of the stamens and pistil using ½-width tape. Cut and taper the stamen ends to prevent too much bulk around the wire. Neaten with tape.

6 Cut the pistil strands to just above the stamens.

7 Dust the stamens with Sunflower Dust Food Colour. This forms the flower centre.

Inner Petals

8 Roll out some Pale Green SFP and cut out two six-petal daisy shapes using the cutter. Soften the edges with a ball tool. Glue the centre of one and place the other on top with the petals positioned in the spaces of those above.

9 Glue the base of the wired stamens and push the petals up and under the prepared pistil/stamens. Squeeze gently to hold them in place then allow to dry.

Outer Sepals

10 Cut a 28-gauge green wire into three equal lengths.

11 Make the outer sepals from Cream SFP using your preferred method for wiring leaves (see pages 19 to 22). Use the rose petal cutter to cut out the shape required.

12 Soften the edges with a ball tool and gently ease and stretch the paste at the top into a gentle point.

13 Vein each sepal with a cornhusk and soften the edges with a ball tool again. Make a gentle curve with your thumb and finger in the middle of the

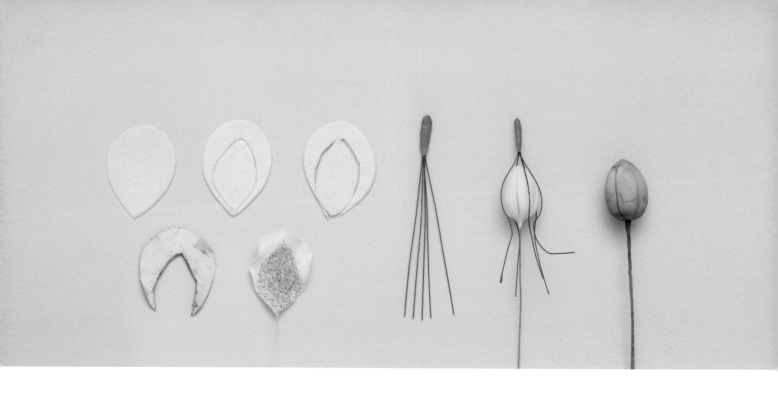

shape. Repeat the process with the other four sepals.

14 To create the mottled effect on the sepals, make a template of the rose petal shape in flower paste, then scribe a smaller petal shape onto the sugar. Cut out and remove this piece.

15 Place the template onto a sepal to mask the outer area. Mix some Cyclamen Dust Food Colour with clear alcohol or water to make a paint. Dip a stiff paintbrush or new, clean toothbrush into the liquid and flick and spray the uncovered area. Repeat on the remaining four sepals. Allow the sepals to semi-dry.

Top tip

It is a good idea to practise this technique first!

Assembling the Flower

16 Using ¼-width pale green floral tape, tape the sepals individually around the prepared centre then continue to tape down the stem.

Buds

17 Roll a piece of Cream SFP into a 2cm (¾") ball, then form this onto a cone-shaped bud.

18 Cut a 22-gauge wire into three equal lengths and make a hook at one end of one wire. Moisten the hook with edible glue and push this into the paste. Re-form the cone shape.

19 Place the bud into a wire cage (see page 18), emboss lines onto the paste then remove the cage. Score lines onto the bud with a craft knife.

20 Dust the base with Leaf Green Dust Food Colour and the tip with Cyclamen. Allow to dry.

Leaves

21 Use the templates to make the leaves, following your chosen method of wiring (see pages 19 to 22).

22 Place each leaf onto the board and use the pointed end of a Dresden tool held at an angle to mark the serrations on the edges of the leaves. Soften the edges with a ball tool and vein the leaves using the Great Impressions Hellebore Leaf Veiner.

23 Dust with a mixture of Leaf Green and Holly/Ivy Dust Food Colours with a touch of Cyclamen.

24 Repeat to make as many leaves as required in different sizes. They usually grow in groups of five on each stem: one large, two medium and two small.

25 Steam the leaves to set the colour then dip into ¼-strength glaze and allow to dry.

26 To assemble the leaves, start with the largest leaf then tape the next size down underneath on either side of this. Finally, add the smaller petals on either side again.

Larches are conifers growing from 15 to 50 metres tall. Although the large tree is a conifer it is also a deciduous tree, losing its leaves every year. The cones are small and the foliage is needle-like green shoots.

Larch Cones

(Boldness) Genus: Larix

Materials

SK Professional Dust Food Colours:
Bulrush, Holly/Ivy

SK Professional Paste Food Colour:
Bulrush

SK Sugar Florist Paste (SFP): White

Equipment

22-, 26- and 28-gauge floral wires:
green

Floral tape: dark green, brown

Six-petal flower cutters: nos. N5-N8
(OP)

Basic edibles and equipment (see page 16)

Needles

1 Break a length of green floral tape approximately 30cm (12") long and stretch it to release the glue. Cut this lengthways into four long, narrow pieces.

2 Break (rather than cut off) pieces approximately 10cm (4") long to preserve the points at the ends.

3 Cut a 28-gauge green floral wire into three equal lengths. Place six to eight strands of tape across one end, approximately 5cm (2") down the wire, fold the wire over the strands and twist the wire to hold the strands in place.

4 Repeat the process to make several of these for one twig.

Cones

5 Colour some White SFP with Bulrush Paste Food Colour to make a warm brown colour.

6 Cut a 26-gauge wire into three equal pieces. Make a tiny hook at one end of a piece of wire and glue this.

7 Make a tiny, oval-shaped cone of the brown SFP, push the glued wire into it, then reshape it. Make

several of these as they will be the anchor point on which the scales of the cones will be attached. Allow them to dry.

8 To make the scales use the six-petal cutters, nos. N5 to N8. Thinly roll out some of the brown SFP on a greased area of the board and cut out the N8 six-petal flower shape. Place this onto the foam pad and gently soften the tips with a ball tool.

9 Brush a very small amount of edible glue in the centre and push the petals (scales) up the wire to enclose the cone lightly.

10 Repeat this again with the same cutter but place the scale shape in the gaps between the previous shape, leaving the scales open slightly.

11 Repeat the same process using the N7 cutter.

12 Make a very tiny ball of paste and flatten it slightly; this will act as a spacer to help separate the petal shapes. Place a touch of glue on it and push it

up the wire. Stick it under the previous scales.

13 Repeat the process with another N7 size, making sure the scales are positioned in between the previous set and the spacer is not visible.

14 Repeat the process once more with another N7 size and add a spacer beneath.

15 Cut out an N6 size; if you want to make a larger cone, make two and remember to use a spacer in between each set. As the scales get larger, slightly increase the size of the spacer but always make sure it is not visible.

16 Use the N5 cutter to enlarge the scales further. Make two sets with a spacer between each.

Top tip

You can adjust the sizes and numbers of scales you use to make larger or smaller cones.

17 Now decrease the size by adding a N7 set of scales followed by another N7 so the cone becomes oval shaped.

Assembly

18 Cut a 20-gauge wire in half and cut a piece of brown floral tape to ½-width. Tape the top of the wire approximately three to four times around the same place to create a bud shape, then continue to tape 2.5cm (1") down the wire.

19 Tape a set of pine needles and a cone onto the wire.

20 Continue to tape down another 5cm (2") and add more needles and another cone.

21 Continue taping down the wire, varying the space between the needles and cones on the wire.

22 Bend the wire with pliers to create a more natural look and score the tape with a craft knife to rough it up. Finally, dust areas with Bulrush and Holly/Ivy Dust Food Colours.

Copper Beech is a large, deciduous tree reaching heights of over 40 metres. The leaves are a warm bronze colour when young, maturing to a deep purple in the summer and turning golden brown in the early autumn.

Copper Beech Leaves

(Prosperity) Genus: Fagus

Materials

SK Confectioners' Glaze

SK Professional Designer Dust Food Colours: Etruscan Brick, Smoky Haze

SK Professional Dust Food Colour: Cyclamen

SK Professional Paste Food Colours: Chestnut, Poinsettia

SK Sugar Florist Paste (SFP): Bulrush

Equipment

Floral tape: brown

22- and 28-gauge floral wires: green

SK Glaze Cleaner (IPA)

Rose leaf cutters: set of 3 (FMM)

SK Great Impressions Chestnut Leaf Veiners: small (4cm), large (9cm)

Basic edibles and equipment (see page 16)

Leaves

1 Colour some Bulrush SFP with Chestnut and Poinsettia Paste Food Colours until you have a rich bronze colour.

2 Cut a 28-gauge green floral wire into three equal lengths.

3 Make the leaves using the bronze coloured paste, following your chosen method for wiring the leaves (see pages 19 to 22). Cut out the leaf using the smallest rose leaf cutter.

4 Vein the leaf using the small chestnut leaf veiner and allow to semi-dry. Place it

into a polythene bag, leaving the bag
slightly open, whilst making the others.

5   Make several leaves in the same
way using the medium leaf cutter.
Repeat the process with the large
cutter, this time using the larger veiner:
the veins open out as the leaf gets
larger.

6   Dust all the leaves with a mixture
of Etruscan Brick, Smoky Haze and a
touch of Cyclamen Dust Food Colours
on the top, then dust the back with
Leaf Green.

7   Steam the leaves to set the colour,
then dip into ¼-strength confectioners'
glaze. Allow to dry.

Assembly

8   Cut a 22-gauge wire in half. Using
⅓-width brown floral tape, tape the
top of the wire two or three times in
the same area to create a slender bud
shape.

9   Continue to tape further down the
wire and introduce a small leaf. Add
another small leaf below the first one
on the opposite side.

10   Continue taping down the stem,
alternating the leaves and increasing
their sizes.

11   Make three stems of different
lengths.

Pyracantha is a dense, spiny, evergreen shrub, with long-lasting red berries in the autumn and highly scented creamy flowers in May.

Pyracantha (Firethorn) Berries

Family: Rosaceae

Materials

SK Confectioners' Glaze

SK Professional Dust Food Colours: Holly/Ivy, Leaf Green, Poinsettia

SK Professional Paste Food Colours: Bulrush, Nasturtium

SK Sugar Florist Paste (SFP): Pale Green, Pale Peach

Equipment

Floral tape: brown

33-gauge floral wires: green

Leaf template (see page 173)

Basic edibles and equipment (see page 16)

Leaves

1 Cut a 33-gauge green floral wire into four equal pieces. Make the tiny, long leaves from Pale Green SFP using your preferred method (see pages 19 to 22). Use the templates to cut out the leaves. You will need to make approximately seven leaves for each bunch of berries.

2 Dust the leaves with Leaf Green and Holly/Ivy Dust Food Colours. Pass through steam to set the colour.

3 Dip the leaves into ¼-strength confectioners' glaze and allow to dry.

Berries

4 Add a tiny amount of Nasturtium Paste Food Colour to a small ball of Pale Peach SFP.

5 Cut a 33-gauge green wire into five pieces. Make a tiny hook at the end of each one.

6 Form a very tiny piece of the peach paste into a ball, brush a small amount of glue on the hook and push the wire into the paste. Re-form the ball shape. Repeat to make as many berries as required.

7 Dust the berries with a mixture of Poinsettia and Nasturtium Dust Food Colours then dip into confectioners' glaze.

8 To make a tiny calyx shape, roll a pinhead-sized piece of Bulrush SFP into a ball. Push the point of a CelStick into the formed ball and push this into the berry whilst the glaze is still tacky. Allow to dry.

Assembly

9 Using ¼-width brown floral tape, tape eight to ten berries together, leaving 2.5cm (1") of wire showing beneath the berries.

10 Tape leaves of different sizes in a cluster at the base of the berries.

11 Tape the bunches onto a 22-gauge wire for use in a spray or arrangement. Some sprays have two or more sets of berries.

For the Arrangement

3 stems of Montbretia, 19 buds per stem

13 Montbretia flowers

3 Hellebore flowers

3 Hellebore buds

2 Hellebore leaves

5 larch cones

25 copper beech leaves

10 Pyracantha berries

5 Pyracantha leaves

Stay Soft

Decorative glass dish

Before you start to assemble the arrangement, stick a ball of Stay Soft into the container to allow it to set off. Lay out the flowers (including any spares) on a soft cloth and have wire cutters, floral tape and long tweezers to hand.

Place a set of hellebore leaves at the back and one diagonally opposite it in the front of the dish. Next, place the Montbretia leaves opposite each other, diagonally in the Stay Soft.

Add two stems of beech leaves, one on either side.

Place the larch cones to one side and the Pyracantha berries to the other side at the base.

Next, place the Montbretia sprays in front of and over their leaves and one at the side to create a triangular shape.

Finally, add the hellebore bud off-centre and then the three hellebore flowers at the front.

Use the pliers to adjust the arrangement as required, making sure the Stay Soft is not visible.

Top tip

Always allow plenty of time to assemble a spray or arrangement so that you can make sure the flowers look their best.

Nothing would be done at all if one waited until one could do it so well, that no one could find fault with it.

Cardinal Newman

Sophisticated Style

Cattleya orchids were the earliest of the showy tropical epiphytic orchids to be grown and flowered in cultivation. There are many species of Cattleyas, which are native to Mexico and central and southern America. Their colours range is from white, pink and yellow to green, purple and red.

Cattleya Orchid

(Delicate beauty) Genus: Cattleya

Materials

SK Sugar Florist Paste (SFP): Pale Yellow, White

SK Professional Dust Food Colour: Daffodil

Equipment

Apple tray

Cattleya orchid cutter set: large (TT)

24-, 26-, 28-gauge floral wires: white

Scriber

Petal veiner/friller tool: no. 12 (JC)

Basic edibles and equipment (see page 16)

Column

1 Cut a 26-gauge white floral wire into three equal parts. Make a tiny hook at one end of a wire with pliers.

2 Roll a 6mm (¼") ball of Pale Yellow SFP and shape this into a cone.

3 Lightly glue the hooked end of the wire, then push the hook into the pointed end of the cone.

4 Place the bulbous end of the cone against your index finger and gently push the small end of a ball tool into the top to hollow it out and thin the sides. Remove the ball tool then press the flat end of the Dresden tool down the length of the paste to hollow out an indentation down the cone and thin the sides.

5 Place the ball tool back into the cone, hold it gently then indent two lines into the tip with the Dresden tool. Reshape into a point then allow the column to dry.

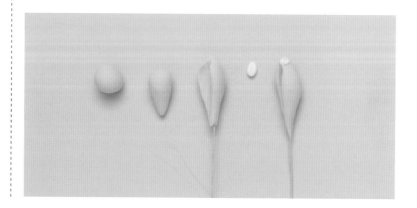

6 Take a tiny, pinhead-sized piece of White SFP and form this into a ball. Moisten the tip of the column and stick it on, then indent it with a scriber to form a tiny line in the middle.

Labellum (Throat)

7 Roll out some White SFP and cut out the throat with the frilly cutter. Place this onto a foam pad and soften the edges with a ball tool.

8 Place the shape onto the board and vein and texture the surface with the veiner/friller tool, pressing fairly firmly to make the markings.

9 Place the shape back onto the foam pad and frill the top and side edges, but not the pointed end.

10 Make a paint by mixing Daffodil Dust Food Colour with a little clear alcohol. Paint this onto an area from the point to halfway down the frilled petal. As the colour dries fast it is possible to assemble this part while the paste is flexible.

11 Take the dried column and brush some edible glue on the edges on either side. Fold the frilled labellum around the column and reshape it so that the column is visible and the frilled area points downwards. Hang this until it holds its shape and is semi-dry.

Sepals

12 Cut a 28-gauge white wire into three equal parts. Use White SFP to make three wired sepals using the thinner orchid petal cutter and your preferred method for wiring (see pages 19 to 22).

13 Soften the edges with a ball tool on a foam pad and vein the surface gently with the veiner/friller tool. Mark a central line down the length of each sepal with the pointed end of the Dresden tool, then pinch the tip.

14 Gently curl two of the sepals backwards and one forwards. Allow to semi-dry.

Petals

15 Cut a 28-gauge white wire into three equal pieces. Roll out some White SFP and cut out the two large petals with the widest cutter. Wire the petals using your chosen method (see pages 19 to 22).

16 Vein the petals gently with the veiner tool, then frill both edges of each petal by pressing firmly on each side with the friller tool.

17 Gently curve the petals backwards and place them into a curved former such as an apple tray to set off.

Assembly

18 Assemble the orchid whilst the component parts are semi-dry and still flexible using ½-width pale green floral tape. Start by taping each of the two frilly petals to either side of the throat: tape one petal first then add the other at the same point but on the opposite side.

19 Place the inward-facing sepal at the top of the throat above the frilly ones and tape this in place. Tape the other two individually on either side at the base of the flower head. Tape down the stem. Allow to dry completely.

20 Pass the orchid through steam to set the colour and allow to dry again.

Pastillage Sticks

SK Professional Dust Food Colours: Bulrush, Chestnut

250g packet SK Pastillage

Basic edibles and equipment (see page 16)

1 Make up the pastillage according to the instructions on the packet.

2 Roll a 2.5cm (1") ball of pastillage then place this onto a foam pad and roll into a long, thin length measuring approximately 30cm (12"). Rolling the paste on a foam pad helps to keep the pastillage even and straight down its length. Trim to size if needed and roll the ends into a neat point.

3 Repeat the process to make more sticks in varying lengths. Allow all the sticks to dry.

4 When dry, dust the sticks with Bulrush and Chestnut Dust Food Colours to create a wood effect.

For the Cake

25cm (10") square cake

35cm (14") square cake drum

1.5kg (3lb 5oz) pale green sugarpaste

5 white Cattleya orchids

24-gauge floral wires: white

10 to 15 pastillage sticks dusted with Bulrush and Chestnut Dust Food Colours (or airbrushed with Liquid Food Colours)

Large posy pick

Pastillage sticks

5 or 6 raffia skeins

1.44m (4' 9") 15mm width ribbon: white

Cut two 24-gauge white wires into three pieces each. Tape a piece of wire under each orchid to strengthen the stems. Tape three orchids together with one higher than the other two, then tape down the wires. Cut the ends of the wires straight.

Tape the remaining two orchids individually.

Cover the cake and cake drum with sugarpaste (see pages 168 to 172) and place the cake centrally on the drum. Fill the posy pick with sugarpaste and mark its position on one corner of the cake (do not push into the cake yet). Glue one side of the pastillage sticks and place them randomly onto the cake from this corner, leaving an area where the posy pick will be. Allow to dry.

Carefully hold the base of the orchids with pliers and push the wires into the posy pick. Next, still holding the pliers, push the orchids into position on the cake. If some of the sticks break, replace them with spares.

Tie the raffia around the base of the cake and position the remaining orchids beside the cake under the raffia. Secure them in place with edible glue or push them into a posy pick and insert this into the side of the cake.

Attach a length of white ribbon onto the board edge with non-toxic glue (see page 171).

Creativity requires the courage to let go of certainties.

Erich Fromm

Iris Inspiration

The Dutch Iris takes its name from the Greek word for rainbow due to the many colours attributed to the species. It is one of the most beautifully shaped bulbous flowers, tall and elegant. This particular variety is the Professor Blaauw blue iris.

Dutch Iris

(Inspiration) Family: Iridaceae

Materials

SK Professional Dust Food Colours: Bluebell, Daffodil, Edelweiss, Violet

SK Professional Paste Food Colour: Leaf Green

SK Sugar Florist Paste (SFP): Holly/Ivy, White

Equipment

Apple tray or former

Bract and leaf templates (see page 173)

Cornhusk

Dutch Iris cutter set (TT)

Floral tape: light green

20-, 26-gauge floral wires: white

SK Great Impressions Dutch Iris Veiners

Kitchen roll

Paintbrush: no. 2

Petal veiner/friller tool: no. 12 (JC)

Basic edibles and equipment (see page 16)

Standard Petals

1 Cut a 26-gauge white floral wire into three equal lengths.

2 Knead some White SFP and make a wired petal using your chosen method (see pages 19 to 22). Cut out the slim petal shape using either the cutter or template.

3 Lightly dust the veiner with cornflour. Place the petal between the two halves of the veiner and press firmly: if any paste is squeezed out of the sides, press the veiner tightly and remove this with your fingers or cut off with small, sharp scissors.

4 Place the petal onto a foam pad. Gently soften the edges with a ball tool, then use a Dresden tool to mark a central vein down the length of the petal. Pinch the tip.

5 Softly run your finger and thumb up the sides of the petals to create movement.

6 Repeat the process to make another two petals, hang them upside-down and allow them to semi-dry.

7 Dust the petals with a mixture of Bluebell, Violet and Edelweiss Dust Food Colours. Use a darker colour at the base of the petals by adding more Bluebell dust to the mixture. Make the petals lighter in colour towards the top.

Fall Petals

8 Cut a 26-gauge white wire into three equal lengths.

9 Roll out some White SFP and make three wired petals using your preferred method (see pages 19 to 22). Cut out the petals using the widest cutter.

10 Place each petal in turn into the veiner as before and press firmly. The veiner will leave a thick ridge down the centre.

11 Frill the rounded edges of each petal with the friller tool to give it more movement.

12 Place the petals in a curved position in an apple tray or curved former and allow to semi-dry.

13 Dust down the centre of each petal with Daffodil Dust Food Colour using a no. 2 paintbrush to approximately halfway down the petal.

14 Roll out some White SFP and cut out a similar shape to the yellow dusted area. Place this over the yellow area to mask it off, then dust around the edge of the covered yellow centre with a mixture of Bluebell, Edelweiss and Violet. Remove the mask paste.

Crest Petals

15 Grease the board with white vegetable fat. Roll out the paste slightly thicker than usual because the veiner creates a deep vein and requires more bulk for a better effect.

16 Cut out the petal using the cutter with the two pointed tips. Vein the petal in the veiner then soften the edges with a ball tool. There is no need to wire these petals.

17 Place the petal onto a foam pad with the ridge facing upwards. Put the ball tool on the point of one of the tips, press gently and move the ball tool back to the main petal; this pressure will cause the tip to be pulled up. Repeat the process with the other tip. Pinch along the ridge if necessary to maintain the shape, support if required and leave the petal to set off.

18 Dust the petal with a mixture of Bluebell and Edelweiss Dust Food Colours. Add some Violet to the mixture to soften the colour and brush this towards the edges of the petals.

19 Using very little edible glue, glue the underside of the edges, excluding the tips. Stick the crest petal to fit over the fall petal from the wire end forwards. Make sure that the tips are raised upwards and that the fall petals point downwards.

Assembly

20 Use ½-width light green floral tape to tape the standard upright petals together, adding one at a time.

21 Next, tape each of the combined fall and crest petals individually between the standard ones.

22 Add a 20-gauge wire underneath the flower for more support (as it will be standing in the arrangement) and tape it in place.

Bracts

23 The iris has pointed, leaf-like bracts which are attached down the stem. To make them, mix some Leaf Green Paste Food Colour into some Holly/Ivy SFP to make a mid-green colour.

24 Roll out the paste and cut out the bract shape using the cutting wheel; you can do this freehand or using the templates as a guide. Start by making a small one approximately 5cm (2") long which will fit at the base of the flower head in a vertical position with the tip overlapping the base of the flower.

25 Vein the bract with a cornhusk and indent a central vein with a Dresden tool.

26 Glue this bract and attach it under the flower head.

27 Repeat this method to make more bracts: you will need two or three per stem, each one slightly longer than the first.

28 Attach the remaining bracts further down the stem and opposite each other.

29 Make three long leaves using the whole length of a 22-gauge floral wire, following your chosen method for making wired leaves (see pages 19 to 22).

30 Vein the leaves down their length with a cornhusk and mark a central vein with a Dresden tool.

31 Allow the leaves to dry in a gentle curve.

32 Brush the bracts and leaves with ¼-strength confectioners' glaze or spray with edible varnish.

Top tip When you are making an iris it is useful to know that the flower is made up of three parts: the upright petals (standards), the drooping petals (falls) and the wing-like petals (crests) which are connected to the fall petals.

These wonderful, dark green, glossy leaves can be used to accompany any arrangement and showcase the flowers for a truly stunning effect.

Philodendron Leaves

Family: Araceae

Materials

SK Professional Dust Food Colour: Holly/Ivy

SK Sugar Florist Paste (SFP): Holly/Ivy

Equipment

22-gauge floral wire: green

SK Great Impressions Philodendron Leaf Veiner: Wide

Leaf template (see page 174)

Basic edibles and equipment (see page 16)

1 Cut a 22-gauge green floral wire into two equal pieces.

2 Make the leaf from Holly/Ivy SFP, following your chosen method (see pages 19 to 22).

3 Cut out the leaf shape using the template and a cutting wheel. Trim into shape if necessary with fine scissors.

4 Vein the leaf with the philodendron leaf veiner and soften the edges with a ball tool.

5 Place the leaf onto crumpled kitchen roll to create movement. Allow the leaf to set off, then dust it with Holly/Ivy Dust Food Colour. Repeat this process to make as many leaves as required.

6 Steam the leaves to set the colour and then glaze them with ½-strength confectioners' glaze. Hang upside down and allow them to dry completely.

Contorted willow branches make a great addition to arrangements, giving a light and airy feel to the display. You can tape in buds or leaves on the branches to create different effects depending on the arrangement.

Contorted Willow

Genus: Salix

Materials

SK Professional Dust Food Colours: Bulrush, Vine

SK Sugar Florist Paste (SFP): Pale Green

Equipment

Floral tape: brown

20-, 30-gauge floral wires: green or white

PVA glue

Basic edibles and equipment (see page 16)

Branches

1 Take five or seven full-length 20-gauge floral wires; they will be covered with tape so can be green or white.

2 Cut some floral tape into ½-width lengths and tape down the wires. Twist just the top of a length of tape then add this above the top of the wire and tape down the length. This will create a finer point on the branch.

3 To make a longer branch, add a further length of wire by taping another wire alongside the first one, overlapping the wires by approximately 5cm (2"). You may need to use more tape to strengthen the join.

Buds

4 Cut a 30-gauge floral wire into five small pieces and make a tiny hook at one end of each piece.

5 Make tiny green cones of Pale Green SFP for the buds. Take a wire, glue the hook and push it into a cone. Allow this to dry.

6 Repeat the process to make two or three buds per branch. Tape the buds down the length of the branches at intervals. For a thicker branch, add more tape over the original tape.

Small Branches

7 Cut a few wires to different lengths, tape them as before and add them to the main piece to make branches.

8 Twist and bend the wires into interesting shapes. Repeat to make as many twigs as required to fill out a display. For the arrangement shown here you will need to make three twigs with branches.

For the Arrangement

3 iris flowers

3 iris leaves

3 branches of contorted willow

3 philodendron leaves

Flat china dish

Small, white pebbles or sugared almonds

Stay Soft: white

PVA or edible glue

This simple arrangement can be presented on a flat dish. Glue some Stay Soft (or pastillage if preferred) into the dish to hold the arrangement firmly in place.

Push the contorted willow into the Stay Soft in the dish first to establish the height and width of the display. Place three irises at different heights in front of these, with the iris leaves around and below the flower heads. Place the three philodendron leaves at the base of the arrangement.

Cover the pastillage or Staysoft with either sugared almonds or small, white pebbles, stick them in place with some glue and scatter some around the dish.

The richness I achieve comes from Nature, the source of my inspiration.

Claude Monet

Dainty and Delicate

Pear blossom appears in the spring as a mass of pretty white flowers that hang in clusters on the trees, making a magnificent display. These delicate little flowers could be used as filler flowers or individually in an arrangement.

Pear Blossom

(Lasting friendship) Genus: Pyrus

Materials

SK Professional Dust Food Colours: Cyclamen, Edelweiss, Vine Green

SK Sugar Florist Paste (SFP): Holly/Ivy, White

Equipment

Blossom cutter: N5 (OP)

30-gauge floral wire: green

General leaf cutter: small (TT)

SK Great Impressions Rose Leaf Veiners

Piece of food-grade foam sponge

PVA glue

Small calyx/jasmine cutter (FMM)

Very fine stamens: white

Basic edibles and equipment (see page 16)

Centre

1 Cut a 30-gauge green floral wire into four pieces.

2 Take five very fine (tiny) stamens and cut them in half through the centre. Dust the tips with Leaf Green Dust Food Colour.

3 Stick the stamens to the top of a wire with PVA glue and allow to dry. This forms the pistil.

4 Cut a further 13-15 stamens in half as before, then dust the tips with Cyclamen Dust Food Colour.

5 Use PVA glue to stick the Cyclamen coloured stamens around and just below the pistil and allow these to dry.

6 Cut off the excess stamen threads at an angle. This helps to stagger the bulk when taping.

7 Cut a small piece of light green floral tape into four lengths. Use one of these to tape around the base of the prepared stamens/pistil.

Flowers

8 Form a pea-sized piece of White SFP into a ball. Flatten it and pinch out the edges, then roll out the paste around the outside to form a tiny bump in the middle (see the Mexican hat method on pages 16 to 17).

9 Place the blossom cutter over the bump and cut out the flower shape. Place this onto a foam pad and gently soften the edges with a ball tool. Then, using the same tool, cup each petal on a piece of foam sponge.

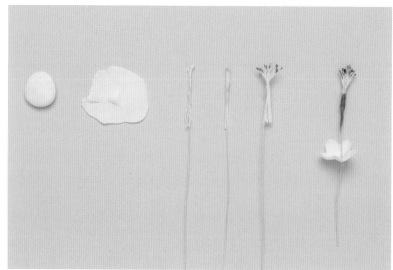

10   Push the prepared centre down through the middle of the flower.

11   Mix a small amount of Holly/Ivy SFP with some White SFP to lighten the colour. Roll out the paste and cut out a small calyx with the cutter.

12   Glue the base of the flower and attach the calyx underneath it.

13   Use ¼-width light green floral tape to tape down the stem.

14   Repeat the method so far to make further flowers as required; you will need to make approximately five to seven flowers per cluster.

Buds

15   To make the buds, roll a tiny piece of White SFP into a ball. Cut a 30-gauge wire into four and make a tiny hook at one end of each wire. Glue a hooked wire and push it into the ball.

16   Mark five indentations on the top of the bud with a craft knife.

17   Cut out a calyx as before, then glue the base of the bud and place the calyx underneath and around it.

18   Tape the stem in the same way as for the flower. Repeat the process to make three to five buds per cluster.

19   Dust the calyces with a mixture of Holly/Ivy and Edelweiss Dust Food Colours to make a grey-green colour.

Leaves

20   Cut a 30-gauge green wire into four equal lengths.

21   Use the same coloured paste as the calyces to make the leaves following your chosen method (see pages 19 to 22). Cut out the leaves with the small to medium leaf cutters. Use the thin end of the cutter as the top of the leaf and not the rounded end as normal.

22   Vein the leaves with the rose veiner then dust them with a tiny amount of Holly/Ivy mixed with Edelweiss Dust Food Colour.

23   Allow them to dry and then pass them through steam to set the colour.

24   Repeat to make around five leaves per cluster of flowers.

Assembly

25   Using ¼-width light green floral tape, tape two flowers together then add two or three to make a cluster of the small flowers and buds in an arch shape. For the arrangement shown you will need to make three little bunches of these.

26   Finally, add approximately five leaves under the bunches of flowers and buds.

Top tip

Ensure that you cut away the stamen ends at a tapered angle to prevent excess bulk when taping the base of this tiny flower. This applies to any centre with multiple stamens in the method.

Jasmine is a beautiful flowering vine with a heady aroma. There are some 200 species of jasmine – the flowers are usually white, sometimes flushed with pink or yellow, but can also be bright yellow or pale pink.

Jasmine

(Grace and elegance) Genus: Jasminum

Materials

SK Professional Dust Food Colours: Edelweiss, Leaf Green, Vine

SK Professional Paste Food Colour: Leaf Green

SK Professional Pastel Dust Food Colour: Pastel Pink

SK Sugar Florist Paste (SFP): Pale Green, White

Equipment

30-gauge floral wire: green

Jasmine cutter (OP)

Leaf cutters: small (TT) (optional)

Basic edibles and equipment (see page 16)

Buds

1 Cut a 30-gauge wire into four equal pieces and make a tiny hook at one end of each piece.

2 Form a tiny ball of White SFP into a sausage shape. Dip the hook into edible glue and feed a wire into the paste.

3 Place the paste onto a foam pad and gently roll it to elongate the paste down the wire, leaving the tip a bulbous shape. The length of the paste should be approximately 3cm (1¼"). Make 25 to 30 buds altogether.

Flowers

4 Cut a 30-gauge wire into four equal pieces. Make a tiny hook at one end of each piece.

5 Make a cone of White SFP approximately 3cm (1¼") long, as for the buds. Flatten or cut off the bulbous tip.

6 Roll out a small amount of White SFP and cut out a small calyx-shaped flower. Place onto a foam pad and cup the centre. Lightly glue the flattened paste at the end of the wire, stick the flower onto this and press into the centre with a CelStick.

Colouring

7 Mix some Pastel Pink Dust Food Colour with some Edelweiss to make it slightly paler. Dust the buds with this then dust the base with Vine.

8 Dust underneath the head of the flower with the pale pink dust; the top of the flower should remain white. Dust the base of the flower with Vine.

Leaves

9 Cut two or three 30-gauge wires into four equal pieces.

10 Make the leaves using your preferred method (see pages 19 to 22)

and cut them out either using the cutters or freehand using a cutting wheel. If you are cutting them freehand, make sure they are long and slender. You will need to make several leaves in varying sizes, starting very small and increasing to 2.5cm (1").

11 Vein the leaves using a scriber then soften the edges with a ball tool to create movement.

12 Dust the leaves with a mixture of Vine and Leaf Green Dust Food Colours and allow to dry. When dry, steam the leaves to set the colour.

13 The leaves grow in sets of five; you will need to make approximately nine sets for the arrangement shown here.

Skeleton leaves can be bought at craft shops and make a decorative accompaniment to a floral display. They are delicate, so handle with care.

To use in an arrangement, wire them first to make them easier to handle. Using a fine paintbrush and PVA glue, brush over the base of the stem, then repeat this on a white floral wire (any gauge). Leave to go tacky and then stick the wire to the leaf base and leave to dry.

For the Arrangement

17 pear blossom flowers

11 pear blossom buds

13 pear blossom leaves

27 jasmine buds

1 lisianthus flower (see page 160)

3 skeleton leaves (wired)

Pearl beads

Glass vase with narrow neck

I have used the flowers here to create a crescent shaped arrangement (see page 26), simply displayed in a small, narrow vase.

Tape the jasmine leaves in sets of five with a single leaf at the start and then the other leaves opposite each other underneath it. Make approximately five sets of these leaves.

Tape three to five buds and one or two flowers together.

Start the stem with small leaves then add some buds. Continue to tape along the wire and add in some more leaves,

then tape up the stem again adding more leaves, buds and flowers.

Make two small stems, starting them in the same way, then add them to the longer one.

Use a lisianthus as the central point of the arrangement then add the clusters of pear blossom stems around the lisanthus and tape them in just below the flower to form a simple arch shape.

Add the trailing stems of jasmine on either side and to complete the display, place the wire skeleton leaves in a triangle shape from the centre.

The world is but a canvas to the imagination.

Henry David Thoreau

Sensational Scarlet

The gerbera was named after the German naturalist, Traugott Gerber. There are vast numbers of cultivars that vary in shape and size; their colours can be soft or vibrant as they grow in white, pink, yellow, orange and red with green or brown centres.

Gerbera

(Innocence, purity, cheerfulness) Family: Asteraceae

Materials

SK Sugar Florist Paste (SFP): Pale Green, Poinsettia

SK Professional Dust Food Colours: Cyclamen, Leaf Green, Poinsettia

SK Professional Paste Food Colour: Leaf Green

SK Professional Pollen Style Dust Food Colour: Apple Green

Equipment

Carnation cutter: 4cm (1½") (OP)

8-petal daisy plunger cutter set (PME)

Fine stamens: white

22-, 20-gauge floral wires: white

Gerbera/sunflower cutter: small (from set of 3) (PME)

Petal veiner/friller tool: no. 12 (JC)

Basic edibles and equipment (see page 16)

Centre

1   Roll a small piece of Pale Green SFP into a ball and flatten it between your finger and thumb to measure approximately 1.5cm (5/8") across.

2   Cut a 22-gauge wire in half. Take a piece of wire and make a small ski stick at one end of the wire (see page 18). Glue this, then push it into the paste and re-form the paste around it, keeping the disc shape. Allow this to dry.

3   When it is dry, brush the surface and the edges of the disc with edible glue and dip it into Apple Green Pollen Dust Colour. Allow this to dry.

4   Roll out some Poinsettia SFP and cut out a flower shape with the carnation cutter. Leave the shape on the board and use a veiner/friller tool to frill and texture the edges.

5   Dust the edges of the petals with Cyclamen Dust Food Colour.

6   Glue the middle of the flower shape then thread the wire through the centre. Push it up and underneath the prepared centre and squeeze the paste around the outside of the flower centre to stick it in place.

7   Repeat the process again to make another layer of petals but do not attach this yet.

8 You can add fine stamens to the flower centre but this is optional. Cut approximately 12 to 14 stamens in half then check the size against the flower: they only need to reach the edge of the petal from the centre. If they are longer than this and go beyond the edge, cut them slightly smaller.

9 Glue the second, unwired flower then use tweezers to place the stamens from the centre to the edge of the petals.

10 Leave this to dry slightly before gluing the base of the previously attached set of petals, then push the petals with the stamens up the wire to stick them underneath the others. Allow to set off.

11 Repeat the process to make another layer of petals and cup the centre of each petal to stretch the shape. Again it is optional to add further stamens. Secure this underneath the other petals to complete the flower centre.

Petals

12 Thinly roll out some more Poinsettia SFP and use the small gerbera/sunflower cutter to cut out one set of petals. Keep the petals in the cutter, turn it over and rub your thumb over the paste to remove any rough edges.

13 Push the petals out of the cutter and onto the board. Press the veiner tool gently on the edges and into the centre to vein and thin the petals. Use the thin end of a Dresden tool to mark two lines on each petal.

14 Allow them to set off slightly so that they are easier to handle. Repeat the process to make another set of petals. Dust the inside of the petals with Cyclamen Dust Food Colour and the outer edge with Poinsettia.

15 Stick the two layers of petals together, with the top petals placed over and in between the base set.

16 Place them gently into a curved former to dry.

Calyx

17 Mix some Leaf Green Paste Food Colour into a small pea-sized piece of Pale Green SFP.

18 Form a small cone of the paste and flatten the wide end. Glue the base of the flower and push the cone up underneath it.

19 Roll out more of the green paste and cut out two daisy shapes using the small (3cm/1⅛") daisy cutter. Cut each sepal into two and stretch each individual sepal gently with a ball tool.

20 Repeat the process with another set of sepals but do not stretch this set; it should be smaller than the previous one.

21 Glue the large, flat daisy shape and place the other set of sepals on top so that they lie between the previous set. The larger shape should be placed directly under the back of the flower with the smaller shape underneath it. Glue the top of the large one and push the petals up underneath the flower. Allow to dry.

Flower Assembly

22 Gerbera flowers grow on thick, single stems. If you are making a standing flower, as in the arrangement, it is advisable to strengthen the stem, so cut a 20-gauge in two and tape this under the flower using ½-width floral tape.

23 To achieve the thick stem, first tape down the length of the wire with ½-width light green tape. Cut a length of kitchen paper into thin strips, wind this around the stem, then tape over it again. Finally, tape down the stem with full-width tape.

24 If the flower does not stay upright on the wire, add a further wire to strengthen it and tape down the length as above to hold it in place.

Pelargoniums are flowering plants that are commonly known as scented geraniums or storksbills. The rounded shape of their leaves lends itself perfectly as a filler to arrangements where the flowers have long stems and few or no leaves.

Pelargonium Leaves

(Gentility) Family: Geraniaceae

Materials

SK Sugar Florist Paste (SFP): Pale Green

SK Professional Dust Food Colours: Leaf Green, Vine, Poinsettia

Equipment

28-gauge floral wires: green

2cm, 3cm, 5cm (¾", 1⅛" and 2") round cutters

SK Great Impressions Pelargonium Leaf Veiners

Petal veiner/friller tool: no. 12 (JC)

Basic edibles and equipment (see page 16)

1 Cut a 28-gauge green floral wire into three equal pieces.

2 Make the leaves from Pale Green SFP following your chosen method for wiring (see pages 19 to 22). Cut out the leaf shapes using different sized round cutters, approximately 2cm, 3cm and 5cm (¾", 1⅛" and 2") in diameter.

3 Vein the leaves with the Great Impressions Pelargonium Leaf Veiners then gently frill the edges with the friller tool to create quite

pronounced undulations around the edges.

4 Dust the leaves with a mixture of Vine and Leaf Green Dust Food Colours, then dust the edges with Poinsettia. Steam the leaves to set the colour.

5 Tape the leaves using ¼-width light green floral tape. Start to tape the smallest leaves first and then graduate to the larger ones down the stem. There are usually between 11 and 13 leaves per stem but obviously more or less can be used.

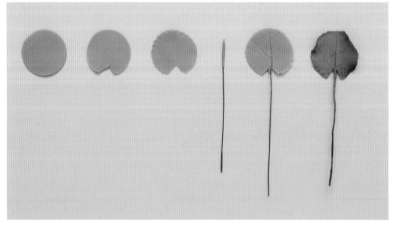

For the Arrangement

5 small, red gerberas

Approximately 30 pelargonium leaves, made into 3 stems (see left)

Stay Soft (or pastillage, if preferred)

SK Sugar Florist Paste (SFP): Black

Black container/dish

Decorative wire: black

Long pliers

Basic edibles and equipment (see page 16)

This arrangement has been placed into a decorative wire support often used in Japanese floral arrangements. I have chosen to use this as it can be stuck to a small cake board and placed directly onto a cake.

Press some StaySoft or very firm pastillage into the base of the dish. Cover the base with Black SFP in keeping with the frame.

First place the stems of pelargonium leaves into the base, two at the front and one standing at the back.

Cut the stems of the gerbera to different lengths, checking the length before cutting them. Make a hole in the Staysoft/pastillage with a paintbrush handle before adding each flower. Use long pliers to push the flowers into position with the tallest at the back, graduating to the smallest at the front. Carefully rearrange the leaves so they cover some of the base.

Finally, add loops of decorative black wire to complement the shape of the dish.

Adopt the pace of nature; her secret is patience.

Ralph Waldo Emerson

Top Tier

Beautiful peonies have graced English gardens since medieval times. The plant, once used as medicine, gets its name from Paeon, the Greek god of medicine and healing. There are numerous varieties and colours of this magnificent plant.

Fringed Peony

(Bashfulness) Species: 'Princess Elizabeth'

Materials

SK Sugar Florist Paste (SFP): Holly/Ivy, Pink, White

SK Professional Dust Food Colours: Cyclamen, Holly/Ivy, Leaf Green

Equipment

Apple tray or former

18-, 28-, 33-, 30-gauge floral wires: white

26-gauge floral wire: green

Large rose petal cutter: 4.5cm (1¾") (TT)

Peony petal, calyx and leaf templates (see page 174)

Basic edibles and equipment (see page 16)

This may seem a very difficult flower for a beginner to make, but it is deceptively simple.

The process for making this flower is based on repetition of the inner fringed petals to the outer frilled ones. It may take some time to make but the end result is worth it and you only need one bloom for impact.

Peonies have stamens, a pistil and seedpods, but as they are not visible I have omitted them.

Centre

1 Cut a 30-gauge white wire into four. Use Pale Pink SFP to make the wired inner petals following your preferred method (see pages 19 to 22). Alternatively, you can try the multi-leaf technique shown here.

2 Roll a sausage of paste then roll this out into a rectangle. Keep the paste at the base fairly thick and roll away from it to thin the top edge. Keep rolling until it is thin. The resulting rectangle should measure approximately 15cm x 7.5cm (6" x 3"). Use a cutting wheel to cut the bottom, top and sides into a reasonably even rectangle.

3 Glue along the thick ridge at the base and place six to eight 30-gauge wires along the glued edge. Fold the paste down over the wires to line up with the base. Press down firmly on the wires with a rolling pin.

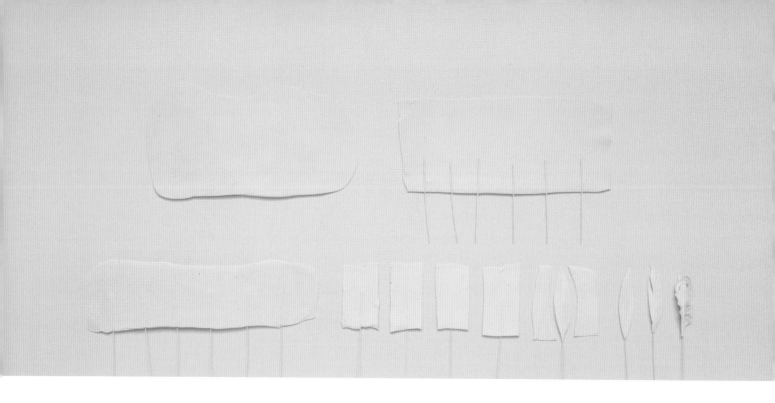

4 Roll over the paste again above the wires to thin the paste further. Make sure you do not roll over the base area too much otherwise the wires will break through the paste.

5 Cut in between the wires with the cutting wheel to create thin, wired rectangles that are ready to use. Place a food-grade polythene bag over them so you can work on one at a time.

6 Take one of the rectangles and thin the edges from the wire outwards with a CelStick. Cut out a long, thin petal shape approximately 3cm (1¼") in length using the template.

7 Cut the tip with scissors to make three points; leave the central one long but cut the other two shorter at different lengths.

8 Soften the edges with a ball tool and curl the petal inwards. Fold the petal in half inwards at the base.

9 Dust the petal with Fuchsia Dust Food Colour on the base and catch the tips with the colour as well.

10 Make approximately 10 to 12 pale pink petals. As they are made let them semi-dry then place them into a polythene bag whilst you make the remaining petals.

11 Start to assemble the petals once they are firm enough to hold their shape. It is important to do this because they become brittle when dry.

12 Use a small length of light green floral tape cut to ⅓-width to tape two petals together. Continue adding others around them as they are made; add two at a time and ensure that they are semi-dry.

13 Make a further set of these petals in White SFP. You will need approximately six to eight but you can make more if you wish to make a bigger bloom. Assemble them as before around the pink petals.

Outer Petals

14 Cut a 28-gauge white wire in half then cut off approximately 2.5cm (1") from each piece of wire.

15 Make the wired outer petals individually using your chosen method (see pages 19 to 22). After you have made each petal, keep it on the board and nip out four or five random cuts from the petal edge using the pointed end of the cutter.

16 Place each petal onto a foam pad and gently stretch each section with a ball tool.

17 Place onto the board again and texture and frill the petal with a veiner/friller tool.

18 Place the petal back onto the foam pad and soften the edges with a ball tool if required.

19 Place the petal into a former and allow to semi-dry in a curved shape.

20 Repeat this method to make 10 to 12 outer petals. Place into a polythene bag to prevent them from drying too quickly whilst you make the others.

21 Once they have set off, use ½-width floral tape to tape five or six petals individually underneath the fringed centre, overlapping the petals as you go. Tape the other petals underneath and in between the first layer. Again it is important not to let the petals get too stiff as they are more likely to break.

Assembling the Flower

22 Pull the mass of wires out, then trim them down the length at an angle to remove some of the bulk.

23 Cut an 18-gauge wire in half and add one piece to the stem to lengthen it. Tape down the stem with light green floral tape.

24 Place the flower into a former if necessary to dry completely.

Buds

25 Cut a 22-gauge wire into thirds. Take one piece and make a hook in one end.

26 Roll a ball of Pale Pink SFP approximately 2cm (¾") in diameter (the size of a small cherry tomato).

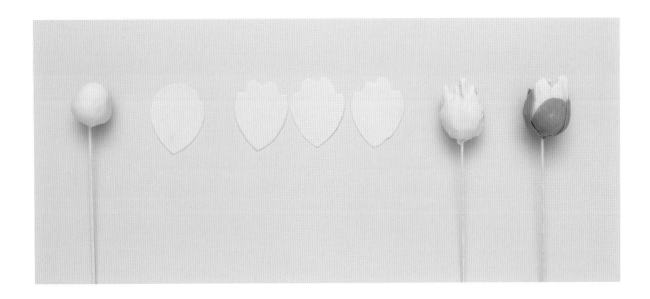

27 Glue the hook in the wire and push it into the paste. Re-form the base then allow to dry.

28 Roll out some Pale Pink SFP and cut out four rose petals using the small rose cutter.

29 Use a veiner/friller tool to texture the petal then soften the edges with a ball tool.

30 Brush the wired ball with edible glue and stick a petal around it. Add another petal on the opposite side. Repeat with the other two petals on either side of the first pair. Allow this to dry.

Top tip

To lessen the weight of the flower, you could use a polystyrene cone or ball instead (see page 9).

Calyx

31 Mix some Holly/Ivy SFP with White SFP to lighten the colour.

32 Roll out the paste and cut out three small rose petal shapes using the template. Soften the edges with a ball tool, brush them with edible glue and stick them under the flower.

33 Cut out two pointed petal shapes using the template or freehand and stick them opposite each other under the flower or on the bud.

34 Tape down the bud with ½-width light green floral tape. Add another wire if the bud is too heavy and tape down the stem again.

35 Repeat to make a calyx for each of the flowers and buds.

Leaves

36 Use the leaf template to make the leaves following your chosen method.

37 Soften the edges with a ball tool and mark a vein down the centre with the Dresden tool. Add more veins from the central one, working outwards from the centre and following the template as a guide. Allow to semi-dry.

38 Dust the leaves with Holly/Ivy and Leaf Green Dust Food Colours, then catch the edges with Cyclamen Dust Food Colour. Allow to dry, then steam them to set the colour.

For the Cake

15cm (6") round cake, covered with white sugarpaste (see pages 168 to 172)

25cm (10") round cake drum, covered with white sugarpaste and trimmed with ribbon (see page 172)

2 peony flowers

3 peony buds

4 peony leaves

2 dowelling rods

String of glass beads or ribbon

Tall-stemmed glass vase

250g (8¾oz) pastillage

Place the covered cake centrally on the covered drum. Allow the cake to firm up before adding the decoration.

For the decoration, push approximately 250g (8¾oz) of stiff pastillage into a tall glass vase. Make a hole in the paste with the end of a CelStick for the peony to be inserted into. Fill the edges of the glass with sugar almonds to hide the pastillage.

Hold the stem of the peony with a pair of pliers and place the peony into the hole. Fill in the area around it with more almonds.

Dowel the cake with two dowelling rods to support the glass vase (see Stacking Cakes on page 172). Stick the vase onto the cake using a thick sugar glue made from sugarpaste mixed with edible glue. It is best to do this when the resting position of the cake has been decided.

Place the glass beads into the vase and over the edge to fall down onto the cake below. Place the other peony at the base of the cake to complete the display.

I have only shown this display on a single cake but it would work well with more peonies on a three-tier stacked cake for a large wedding.

Innovation is the creation of the new or the rearranging of the old in a new way.

Michael Vance

Reflections

Water lilies are plants of exceptional beauty, purity, and mystery often portrayed in paintings by great artists. There are many colours and species of this lovely flower.

Water Lily

(Purity of Heart) Family: Nymphaeaceae

Materials

SK Confectioners' Glaze

SK Piping Gel

SK Professional Dust Food Colours: Daffodil, Edelweiss, Holly/Ivy, Leaf Green, Poinsettia

SK Sugar Florist Paste (SFP): Holly/Ivy, White

Equipment

Cornhusk

Cocktail sticks

Foam sponge pieces

SK Glaze Cleaner (IPA)

Kitchen foil

Kitchen roll

Lily stamens: yellow

Petal former or apple tray

Petal and leaf templates (see page 174)

Set of round cutters: 4cm-6.5cm (1½"-2½")

Basic edibles and equipment (see page 16)

Centre

1 Take approximately 10 to 12 yellow lily stamens and cut them in half. Line up the tips and cut off any excess at the base to make them all level.

2 Use PVA glue to stick the bases together and allow them to dry.

3 Take approximately 15 to 20 stamens and cut them in half as before.

4 Glue the base of these in small bunches first, then attach to the previously glued stamens, making them slightly higher than the first set. Allow to dry.

5 Cut the base off the stamens to make them even then dust them with Daffodil Dust Food Colour.

 If you can't find yellow lily stamens, they can be made using round head stamens with the tips cut off or cut pieces of 33-gauge wire. Lightly brush the stamens or wires with PVA glue and dip into Pale Yellow Pollen Dust Colour. Glue them together as described above.

Petals

6 Thinly roll out some White SFP. Using the template and cutting wheel, cut out a large size petal.

7 Soften the edges with a ball tool on a foam pad then vein the petal on a cornhusk. Gently use the Dresden tool to mark a central vein from the base to the tip.

8 Curl the tip inwards with a cocktail stick and place it into a curved former.

9 Repeat the process to make another seven to nine large petals for the outer layer. Allow these to semi-dry until they hold their shape.

10 Repeat the whole process again with the medium petal and smaller sized petal templates.

11 Do not let the petals dry completely: start to assemble them whilst they are semi-dry. Form a curved shape with kitchen foil and apply some white vegetable fat to the centre of the former to prevent the petals from sticking.

12 Place a 2cm (¾") flat disc of flower paste into the centre of the former. Brush some edible glue onto this.

13 Lilies can have between 18 and 24 petals so you can decide how numerous the petals are. Arrange the largest petals onto the disc so that they overlap each other. Glue the base of each petal if required.

14 Repeat the process with the medium set of petals to create an inner layer, placing these in the spaces between the outer petals. Support them with some kitchen roll or small pieces of foam sponge so that they stand away from the other petals below.

15 There will be a build-up of SFP in the centre of the flower, so push the end of a paintbrush into this to make an indentation. Brush some edible glue into the hole. Hold the prepared centre with tweezers and press it into place.

16 Finally, repeat the assembly process with the smallest petals and glue them into the middle around the central stamens. Support the petals again so that they curl inwards around the stamens. Allow to dry.

17 When the flower is dry, carefully remove the sponge/kitchen paper supports with tweezers.

18 Dust the base with Leaf Green and Poinsettia Dust Food Colours mixed with Edelweiss for the petals.

Brush the edges of the petals with a stronger mix of colour.

19 To add water drops on the petals and leaves, dip a paintbrush into piping gel and place the drops onto the surface. Allow to dry.

Half-open Flower

20 Make the stamen centre as before.

21 Add the petals in layers, as above, but make one or two fewer petals. Again make sure that the petals are semi-dry for assembling the flower.

22 Assemble the flower as before but close the flower up whilst it is drying by placing it into a foil former made into a cup shape.

Buds

23 Make a ball of White SFP approximately the size of a cherry tomato. Form this into a cone and place it onto a cocktail stick.

24 Mark four deep lines from the tip to the base of the cone with a cutting wheel. Mark random fine lines down the cone between them. Dust with a mixture of Poinsettia and Edelweiss Dust Food Colours and allow to dry.

25 Roll out some Holly/Ivy SFP and cut out four petal shapes to fit around the bud for the calyx sepals. Vein these on the cornhusk.

26 Dust one side only with Leaf Green Dust Food Colour, then add a touch of Poinsettia to the edges. Dust the inside with Edelweiss.

27 Glue the base of the white dusted side and stick this around the pink bud as an opening flower.

28 To make an unopened bud, make the cone from Holly/Ivy SFP and mark the paste in the same way as above. Dust with Leaf Green and Holly/Ivy Dust Food Colours with a touch of Poinsettia on the tips.

29 Paint some ½-strength confectioners' glaze onto the buds and allow to dry.

Leaves

30 Roll out some Holly/Ivy SFP and cut out a leaf using the template or a circle cutter. Cut a small 'V' shape into the leaf.

31 Soften the edges with a ball tool on the foam pad. Vein the leaf using a Dresden tool, marking a central vein then curving outwards from the centre.

32 Curl the edges up to create some movement and support these with kitchen roll or foam sponge pieces.

33 Repeat the process to create more leaves in varying sizes, the largest being approximately 6cm (2³/₈"). For the arrangement shown on page 140 you will need to make seven leaves altogether.

34 Allow all the leaves to semi-dry then dust them using Leaf Green and Holly/Ivy Dust Food Colours. Add a touch of Poinsettia around the edges of the leaves.

35 Paint some ½-strength confectioners' glaze onto the leaves and allow to dry.

The Great Reedmace, often known as bulrush, is widespread throughout the UK and grows in the water at the edges of lakes and slow flowing rivers. The spiked flowers develop from June to August, with the beige coloured male flower directly above the darker textured female flower.

Bulrush

(Indiscretion) Family: Typhaceae

Materials

SK Sugar Florist Paste (SFP): Bulrush

SK Professional Pollen-style Dust Food Colour: Russet

Equipment

20-gauge floral wires: white

Basic edibles and equipment (see page 16)

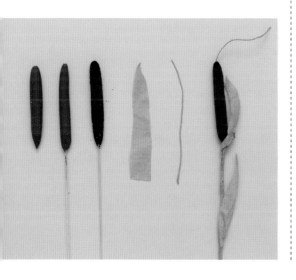

Leaves

1 Cut a 20-gauge white floral wire in half.

2 Roll a ball of Bulrush SFP approximately 2cm (¾") in diameter, then form this into a sausage shape.

3 Brush some edible glue onto one end of a piece of wire and twist the sausage of paste onto this. Roll the paste on a non-stick board until it measures approximately 7.5cm (3") in length. (You can make it longer or shorter if required.) Shape the base by pinching the paste around the wire.

4 Brush some edible glue over the paste and immediately roll in Russet Pollen Dust to cover the paste.

5 Make a hole in the top of the sausage shape with a scriber and allow to dry.

6 Cut a length of beige floral tape to ½-width and tape down the length of the wire under the pollen covered paste.

7 Cut a thin slither of tape and twist this into a thin strand. Glue the hole in the top of the paste and push the strand into it.

8 To make the leaves cut a piece of the tape approximately 10cm (4") long. Cut a point at one end, stretch the tape then place onto a foam pad and use the pointed end of a Dresden tool to stretch and distress the tape. Tape this underneath the sausage shape.

9 Repeat the process to make another leaf and attach it on the opposite side further down the stem. Make three or four leaves and attach them opposite each other.

10 For the display shown on page 140 you will need to make three bulrushes of different heights.

The Marsh Marigold, also known as 'Kingcup', is one of our most ancient plants. It is a member of the buttercup family and thrives near water and ponds.

Marsh Marigold

Species: Caltha Palustris

Materials

SK Professional Dust Food Colours: Daffodil, Vine

SK Professional Pollen-style Dust Food Colours: Pale Yellow

SK Professional Paste Food Colours: Sunflower, Vine, Bulrush

SK Sugar Florist Paste (SFP): Daffodil, Pale Green

Equipment

Emery board (new)

Fine cotton thread: yellow

Five-petal cutters: F9, F10 (OP)

28-gauge floral wire: white

SK Great Impressions Tea Rose Leaf Veiner: 4.5cm (1¾")

Set of round pastry cutters: 2cm, 3cm, 4cm (¾", 1⅛", 1½")

Basic edibles and equipment (see page 16)

Centre

1 Cut a 28-gauge wire into three equal pieces.

2 Spread out two fingers and wind the yellow cotton around them 35 times. Remove the cotton, twist it into a figure of '8' shape and fold this in half to make a loop.

3 Feed one end of a piece of wire through the loop of the cotton and fold it over the cotton. Twist the wire firmly to hold the cotton in place. Repeat this at the other end of the cotton with another wire.

4 Cut the cotton in half through the middle, separating the wires and creating two sets of stamen centres. Cut the cotton down to 7mm (¼"). Wind a piece of cotton around the base of each one (where the wire is twisted around the cotton) to hold the cotton in place.

5 Cut a small length of light green floral tape to ⅓-width. Stretch this and tape the base of the cotton, then continue to tape down the wire.

6 Brush over the cotton tips with an emery board to fluff them up.

7 Open the centre with the end of a paintbrush. Dip a no. 1 paintbrush into Vine Dust

Food Colour and place this into the centre of the stamens to colour the base green.

8 Gently brush the tips of the cotton with edible glue then dip them into Pale Yellow Pollen Dust Food Colour. Separate them to make the centre visible again.

Petals

9 Add some Daffodil SFP to a small amount of Sunflower Paste Food Colour to make the petals.

10 Make a Mexican hat shape (see pages 16 to 17) with just a tiny bump in the middle of the paste. Cut out the flower shape with the F9 five-petal cutter.

11 Turn the flower over and place the bump over the hole in a foam pad. Texture the petals lightly with the veiner/friller tool soften the edges with a ball tool.

12 Remove the flower from the pad and hold it between your fingers. Dip

a scriber into white vegetable fat, push it into the centre of the petals then remove it.

13 Glue the base of the prepared petals and feed the wired stamens through the hole. Secure the petals to the centre and tidy the base around the wire. Allow to set off so that the paste holds its shape.

14 Dust the petals gently with Daffodil Dust Food Colour and the base of the flower with Vine.

Buds

15 Cut a 28-gauge wire into quarters and make a tiny hook at one end.

16 Make a tiny ball of yellow SFP, the same colour as the petals. Glue the hook of the wire and place the ball onto it. Mark five indentations on the top with a craft knife.

17 Dust the base of the bud with Vine Dust Food Colour and the top with Daffodil.

1 full water lily

1 half-open water lily

3 water lily buds

7 water lily leaves

3 bulrushes

2 marsh marigold stems of 4 full flowers, 2 opening flowers and 3 buds

Pebbles made from marbled sugarpaste

Royal icing or thick sugar glue

25cm (10") round display mirror

The arrangement has been assembled in a very simple way to show the beauty of the individual pieces.

Place the water lilies, leaves and buds onto the mirror to one side. Add the bulrushes towards the back and finally place the marsh marigolds in front of the bulrushes. Once you are happy that the arrangement is balanced, secure all the pieces in place with royal icing or a thick sugar glue and support until dry.

Surround the bulrush stems and marigolds with sugarpaste pebbles. To achieve the marbled effect, add some brown paste colour to the white paste but do not blend it in completely. Add streaks of Bulrush for more effect, form into oval shapes, allow to dry and then glaze with confectioners' glaze.

18   For an opening bud, make a bud as above, then roll out some yellow paste and cut out a set of petals with the F10 cutter. Glue the centre and push it up the wire and around the bud. Repeat the dusting as above.

Leaves

19   Mix some Pale Green SFP with Vine Paste Food Colour to make a bright green colour.

20   Roll out the paste and cut out several leaf shapes using the smallest and next size up of the round pastry cutters. Cut out more circles from the remaining paste and cover these with a polythene bag to prevent them from drying too quickly.

21   Using 28-gauge white floral wire, wire the leaves using the 'thin paste on wire' method (see page 21).

22   Serrate the edges of the leaves on the board by pressing the wide end of a Dresden tool at an angle on the edge of the paste.

23   Vein the leaves with the rose veiner, then soften the edges with a ball tool.

Assembly

24   Cut some green floral tape to $1/3$-width. Start taping down the wire of a flower, leave a small length of stem then add an opening bud, another flower and then two leaves.

25   Tape two opening flowers together with one above the other. Leave some stem showing, then tape a leaf below them. Add these to the other flower and buds already taped to form a little branch. Repeat this process with more flowers and buds.

The way to get good ideas is to get lots of ideas, and throw the bad ones away.

Linus Pauling

Old World Charm

Casablanca lilies belong to the lily family and are known for their magnificent blooms and irresistible fragrance. In favourable growth conditions a single bloom can reach 25cm in diameter and grow to over a metre tall. These beautiful flowers are often used in wedding bouquets.

Casablanca Lily

(Celebration) Family: Liliaceae

Materials

SK Sugar Florist Paste (SFP): Bulrush, White

SK Professional Dust Food Colours: Edelweiss, Vine

SK Professional Pollen-Style Dust Food Colour: Russet

Equipment

Apple tray or former

Casablanca lily cutter: 11cm (large) (TT)

Double-edged veining tool: no. 5 (JC) (optional)

Floral tape: dark green

22-.26-gauge floral wires: white

26-gauge floral wire: green

Floral tape: light green

SK Great Impressions Casablanca Lily Veiner: wide

Long, sharp scissors

Basic edibles and equipment (see page 16)

Stamens

1 Cut a 28-gauge white wire into four equal lengths.

2 Using pliers, make a tiny 'T' bar shape by bending the tip of a wire over by 4mm ($^1/_8$"). From the bend, bend the wire by 2mm ($^1/_{16}$") then bend the first part back to the middle so it resembles a 'T' shape (see page 18).

3 Take a pinhead-sized piece of Bulrush SFP and form into a tiny sausage shape.

4 Lightly glue the 'T' and push it into the tiny sausage shape. Re-form the paste around the wire.

5 Make six of these and allow to dry. Lightly glue the stamens then dip them into Russet Pollen Dust Colour.

Top tip Bending the wires can be fiddly, so you can use lily stamens if you prefer. Lightly glue each stamen, dip them into Russet Pollen Dust Food Colour and again leave them to dry.

6 Cut a 22-gauge white floral wire in half, then cut a small amount off the ends to make each one slightly shorter.

7 Take a pea-sized piece of White SFP and form this into a small sausage shape. Glue the top of a piece of wire and feed the sausage shape onto it.

8 Place this onto a foam pad and roll it to thin the sausage of paste. It should be approximately 5cm (2") long so remove any excess paste.

9 Form a rounded tip and then mark three even indentations with a Dresden tool. Allow to dry.

10 Dust the pistil with a mixture of Vine and Edelweiss Dust Food Colours, making the tip slightly darker.

Petals

11 There are six petals for this flower, three large and three narrow. Make a large petal first on a 26-gauge white floral wire using your chosen method for wiring (see pages 19 to 22).

12 Vein the petal with the Casablanca lily petal veiner.

13 Place the petal onto a foam pad. Dip a scriber into white vegetable fat, then place it as flat as possible onto the petal. Lift tiny pieces of the SFP from the base

(wired end) to approximately halfway up. This will represent the tiny hairs on the petal.

14 Soften the edges with a ball tool then stroke the petal on either side from the base upwards to give movement and curl the petal inwards slightly. Finally, curl the tip backwards. Place in an apple tray cup to support the shape until semi-dry.

15 Repeat the process to make another two large petals. When they are semi-dry, place into an open polythene bag to prevent them from drying completely.

16 Make the narrow petals in the same way but without the 'hairs'. Vein each one in the veiner, soften the edges with a ball tool then curl the tip backwards.

17 Dust the base of each petal on both sides with a tiny amount of the pale green dust mixture then allow to semi-dry.

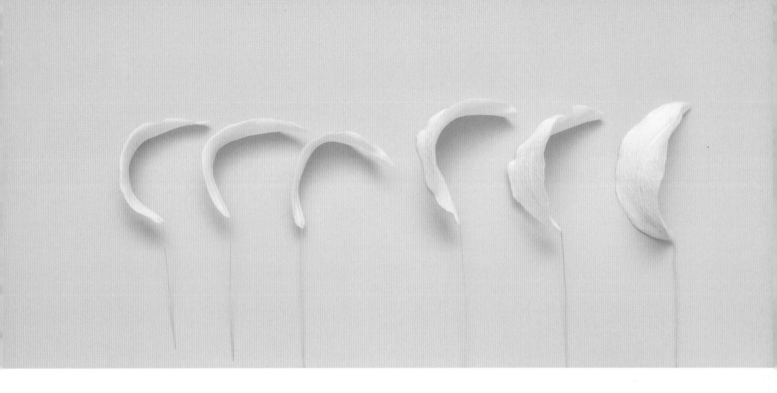

Top tip

It is very important that the flower is assembled whilst the paste is semi-dry as the petals will fit together better.

Assembly

18 Using ½-width light green floral tape, tape the stamens around the base of the pistil in pairs. The stamens should sit just below the pistil.

19 Tape a large petal at the base of the pistil and stamens, then add the other two petals around the centre, ensuring they are taped in firmly.

20 Add the thinner petals individually behind and in the gaps between the large ones, making sure they fit tightly around the flower.

21 Tape down the stem of the lily with full-width light green tape.

Buds

22 Roll a small ball of White SFP 2.5cm (1") in diameter and form this into a tapered sausage 4cm (1½") long.

23 Cut a 22-gauge wire into three equal lengths. Glue the end of one wire and push the tapered sausage onto it, then re-form the base.

24 Mark the tip in three equal parts. Roll a cutting wheel down the length of the bud at each point marked. Repeat this to create a small double line from each point, or use a Jem double-edged veining tool.

25 Dust the base with the pale green dust colour used on the flower.

26 Tape down the length of the wire with full-width light green floral tape.

This handsome tree flourishes in full sun and is native to the Canary Islands. It forms a thick trunk with large, deep green, frond-like leaves. I have made the palm frond using the floral tape method (see page 22). It can be made in sugar but is delicate and not as flexible.

Phoenix Palm

Family: Arecaceae

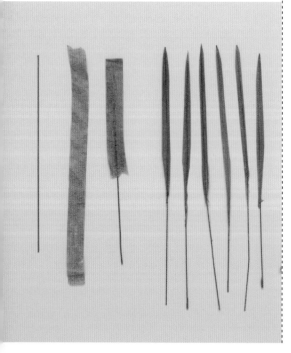

Equipment

26-gauge floral wire: light green

Basic edibles and equipment (see page 16)

Fronds

1 Cut a 26-gauge wire in half.

2 Cut five pieces of light green floral tape, each approximately 10cm (4") long. Stretch the tape gently to increase the length.

3 Place a piece of tape onto a non-stick board. Spread PVA glue onto the surface of the tape.

4 Place a wire at the halfway point of the tape, fold the tape over it and stick it down. Leave it to dry.

5 Repeat the process with more wires and the other pieces of tape.

6 Make slightly larger leaves in the same way by increasing the size of the pieces of tape. The leaves grow in pairs down the stem, so make a few of each size. You will need to make approximately 38 pairs.

7 Once the glue has dried you can cut out the leaf shapes. Using a pair of long, sharp scissors, start at the top of the leaf and cut a point, then cut down the length to shape the leaf on either side of the wire.

Assembly

8 Cut a small piece of light green floral tape to $1/3$-width. Start with the smallest leaf and tape the other small ones below it on either side.

9 Continue down the stem, adding larger leaves below the previous ones in pairs and tapering the shape towards the base. When the palm shape is complete, tape down the stem.

For the Cake

3 Casablanca lilies

1 stem Phoenix palm

15cm (6") heart shaped cake, covered with cream sugarpaste (see pages 168 to 172)

20cm and 25cm (8" and 10") heart shaped cake drums, covered with cream sugarpaste (see page 172)

Long string of pearls

Large posy pick

Place the smaller cake drum on top of the larger one and stick them together. Place the cake to one side of the cake drums and stick it down. You will need approximately 750g (1lb 10½oz) of cream sugarpaste to cover the cake and drums.

The lilies can be placed in the space beside the cake, so they are protected on the board. Mark the position of the flowers halfway along the cake side and just above the base by pushing a CelStick into the cake. Remove the CelStick.

Tape a lily to the base of the Phoenix palm stem then add a few more leaves below this. Use a pair of pliers to place the lily and palm fronds into a large posy pick filled with cream sugarpatse, then push the posy pick into the hole created in the cake, still using the pliers to hold the stem.

Tape another lily and bud together and stick this beside the other lily using thick sugar glue.

Carefully drape a string of pearls over the cake and around the base.

Enthusiasm is excitement with inspiration, motivation and a pinch of creativity.

Bo Bennett

Rose in Bloom

Roses have delighted people throughout the centuries with their wonderful fragrance and form. These amazing flowers look fabulous in sugar flower displays, or simply as a single bloom placed on a cake. Featured in my first book of sugar flowers, it deserves a place once again in this book.

Rose

(Red – Love, Yellow – Joy, Pink – Admiration, White – Purity, Orange – Fascination, Lavender – Enchantment, Peach – Modesty) Genus: Rosa

Materials

SK Confectioners' Glaze

SK Sugar Florist Paste (SFP): Holly/Ivy, White

SK Professional Dust Food Colours: Holly/Ivy, Poinsettia, Vine

Equipment

Apple tray

Calyx cutter: R11 (small, for a small rose) or R11E (large for a life-size rose) (OP)

Cocktail sticks

Five-petal flower cutter: F6C (OP)

Floral tape: dark green

20-, 28-gauge floral wire: white

Foam pads (set of 2) (PME)

SK Glaze Cleaner (IPA)

SK Great Impressions Tea Rose Leaf Veiner: Large

Polystyrene CelBuds (cone shape): size 3 or 4 (CC)

Rose petal cutters: nos. 549, 550 (TT) (only required for a life-size rose)

Rose leaf cutters: set of 3 (FMM)

Tall glass or container

Basic edibles and equipment (see page 16)

There are many methods for making sugar roses – the one shown here is called the 'all-in-one method' using a blossom cutter. It can be used to make roses of any size by varying the size of cutter – this life-size rose looks stunning if you wish to present the flower on its own.

Centre

1 To use the polystyrene cone, make a hole in the base (the large end) with a scriber: this will be where the wire is inserted. Make another hole through the side of the cone just above the base.

2 Cut a 20-gauge white floral wire into two pieces and push one piece into the base of the cone. Push a 28-gauge wire through the side hole and fold down. Now twist the wire around the 20-gauge wire with pliers and cut off any excess wire if necessary. This forms the centre to build your rose on.

3 Repeat these steps to make as many centres as you require for your project in advance.

Top tip The reason for using a polystyrene cone is to make the flower lighter for a larger rose as the sugar can be heavy. If you are making a smaller rose, the centre can be made with flower paste. Use a hooked, 24- or 22-gauge floral wire instead of the 20- and 28-gauge wires.

Petals

4 Grease a section of the board with white vegetable fat then roll out some White SFP quite thinly. Turn the paste over onto an un-greased part of the board and cut out a set of petals using the blossom cutter. Place the petals onto a foam pad and use a ball tool to soften the edges.

5 Brush some edible glue on the cone. Place the petals over a hole in the foam pad then push the end of the wire into the centre of the petals and through the hole in the foam pad. Place the foam pad over a tall glass or container: this frees both of your hands to work on the rose.

6 Apply edible glue onto the cone and halfway up the length of one petal. Wrap one side around the cone, then wrap the other around it. Make sure that the cone is not visible. Miss out the next petal and repeat the process with the third, folding it gently around the first petal and over the join.

7 Brush edible glue onto the base, halfway up on the left-hand side of the remaining three petals. Stick the first of these to the bud at the same level, leaving the right-hand side free and unstuck. Interlock the next petal so that it is tucked under the previous one and repeat this with the final petal.

8 Gently ease the petals downwards, keeping the top of the petals at the same level as the others, and wrap them around the other petals to create a spiral effect.

9 To create an opening rose bud, attach a calyx to the base of the petals at this stage (skip to point 17).

10 Cut out another set of petals for the next layer. Cut away two petals opposite each other then stretch the sides of the remaining three petals with a ball tool (do not lengthen the petals when you stretch them). Soften the edges of each petal with a ball tool and cup them in the centre (see page 17 for details on cupping).

11 Turn the petals over and use a cocktail stick to curl the edges of each petal from the central point at the top at an angle to the middle point on each side. Place the petals in a flower former and leave them to semi-dry so that they hold their shape.

12 Apply edible glue to the base of the opening bud and feed the prepared petals up the wire. Position the petals so that they stand away from the bud slightly. At this point, attach a calyx to the base of the flower to form a half-open rose (skip to point 17).

13 Cut out another set of the petals using the same blossom cutter. Stretch the petals both lengthways slightly and widthways to make them larger. Cup each petal in the centre with a ball tool then turn the blossom shape over and curl the edges of each petal to the centre point with a cocktail stick, as before. Ensure that they will be at the same level as the previous set of petals, then leave in a former to semi-dry so that they hold their shape.

14 Apply edible glue to the base of the half-open rose then thread the end of the wire into the centre of the petals. Turn the flower upside down and gently arrange the outer layer of petals so that they rest over the edges of the second layer of petals, overlapping this set of petals but not completely covering them. Gently press the base of the outer petals to secure them in place but ensure they stand away slightly from the previous layer of petals.

15 Make two layers of five single, wired petals using the two sizes of petal cutters. Wire the petals using your preferred method (see pages 19 to 22) then vein and curl the edges of the petals, as before. Gently curve each petal at the base and allow to semi-dry. Tape the smaller set of petals around the flower using ½-width dark green floral tape, then add the larger set around the outside, overlapping the joins of the first set.

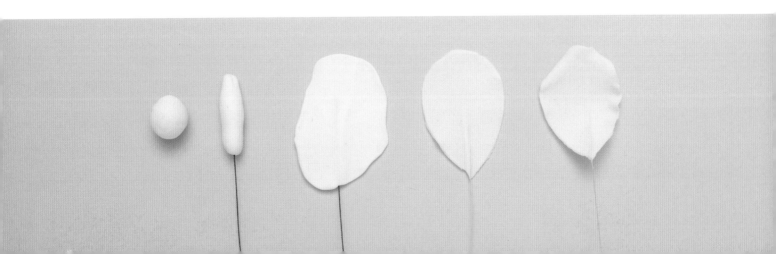

Tape each petal individually in place, then allow to dry completely in a flower former.

16 Dust the centre of the rose with a mixture of Vine and Edelweiss Dust Food Colours.

Calyx

17 Make a Mexican hat shape from Holly/Ivy SFP (see pages 16 to 17).

18 Place the calyx cutter over the bump in the paste and cut out the calyx. Turn the calyx over then press the point of a CelStick in the centre and widen the hole with a ball tool.

19 Dust the inside (top) of the calyx with a mixture of Holly/Ivy and Edelweiss Dust Food Colours. Make two or three tiny cuts into the sides of the sepals using fine scissors, then brush edible glue into the centre of the calyx and thread it up the wire onto the back of the rose. Arrange the sepals so that they curl away from the base of the rose slightly.

20 Brush some confectioners' glaze over the calyx to create a natural sheen. When you have finished, immediately clean the paintbrush with glaze cleaner.

Leaves

21 Roll out some Holly/Ivy SFP and cut out a leaf shape. Vein the leaf with the Great Impressions Tea Rose Leaf Veiner then follow your preferred method to wire the leaf (see pages 19 to 22).

22 Dust the leaf with Holly/Ivy and Vine Dust Food Colours and add touches of Cyclamen on the edges. Steam the leaves and allow to dry.

23 Dip the leaf into ¼-strength confectioners' glaze to create a sheen then allow it to dry again.

24 A stem of rose leaves has one large leaf at the top, two medium leaves below this and then two small leaves. Tape down the leaves for about 2.5cm (1") with green floral tape, then tape them close to the central wire opposite each other down the stem.

Top tip

If you are short of time a wire can be fixed into the paste by heating the hooked end over a naked flame. Once red hot, push the wire into the paste and it will melt and fuse to the sugar immediately. This method can also be used should a flower fall off its wire. However, ensure you take great care and wear protective gloves if attempting this, as the length of the wire will conduct the heat.

For the Arrangement

2 or 3 sets of rose leaves

Single rose

Small vase

The life-size rose can be simply displayed on its own in a small vase or placed on top of a cake. Make a single rose and add two or three sets of rose leaves down the stem. Place the rose into a small vase, tall glass or similar container.

Smaller roses can be made into a rose spray – see Simple Wiring and Arrangements on pages 24 to 27.

There are no failures — just experiences and your reactions to them.

Tom Krause

The Gift

A stylish, tall plant with large funnel-shaped flowers, the colours can be shades of pink to rose, mauve, blue and violet, or white, cream and two-toned colours. The word Eustoma is derived from the ancient Greek word for beautiful.

Eustoma Grandiflorum
(Calming) Common name: Lisianthus

Materials

SK Professional Dust Food Colours: Cyclamen, Edelweiss, Lilac, Violet

SK Professional Pollen Style Dust Food Colour: Pale Yellow

SK Sugar Florist Paste (SFP): Pale Green, Pale Yellow, White

Equipment

Fine pliers

20-, 26-, 28-gauge floral wires: green

24-gauge floral wires: white

Leaf templates (see page 174)

Long tweezers

Paperclip

Petal veiner/friller tool: no. 12 (JC)

Round head stamens: white

Rose petal cutters: 3.5cm, 4.5cm (1³⁄₈", 1¾") (TT)

Basic edibles and equipment (see page 16)

Pistil

1 Cut a 24-gauge white floral wire into three equal lengths. Make a 'T' bar at the top of the wires: to make this, use a pair of pliers to make a bend in the wire no more than 5mm (¹⁄₈") from the end. Hold the bend in the wire again and, with the pliers, pull the wire back to the middle forming a 'T' shape (see page 18).

2 Take a 3mm (¹⁄₈") ball of Pale Yellow SFP and roll it into a tiny oval shape. Place it on a non-stick board. Sparingly glue a 'T' bar made previously and gently push it into the centre of the oval, covering the 'T' part completely with the paste.

3 Squeeze and flatten the ends of the paste, then use tweezers to pinch the centre, making a bow shape. Allow to dry.

4 Lightly glue the paste with edible glue and dip into Pale Yellow Pollen Dust Colour. Allow to dry.

5 Take a tiny piece of Pale Green SFP and roll this into a sausage. Glue the base of the yellow pistil and roll the paste around the top of the wire. Thin the paste on the wire and remove any excess paste if necessary.

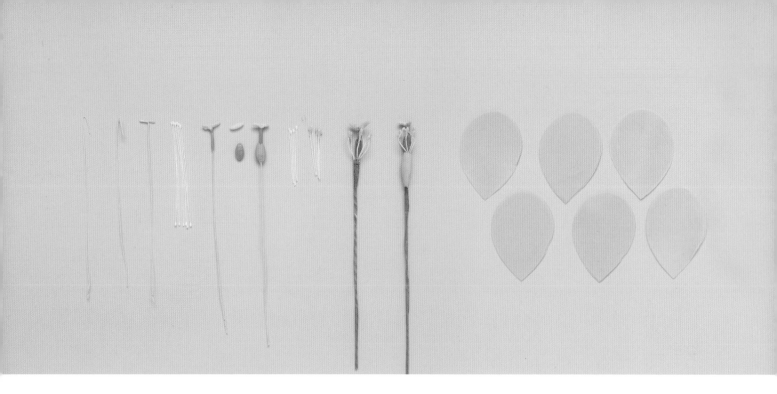

6 Take another small piece of Pale Green SFP and form this into an oval. Glue the wire under the base of the pistil, push the wire into the tiny oval and re-shape it. Allow to dry.

Stamens

7 Cut six round head stamens in half, lightly glue the tips and then dip them into Pale Yellow Pollen. Allow to dry.

8 Glue the stamens to the base of the prepared pistil with PVA glue. Use ¼-width light green floral tape to cover the stamens and wire. Once dry, separate the stamens and then gently curl them inwards with tweezers.

9 Cut a 22-gauge wire into thirds and then tape a piece of wire underneath the centre with ¼-width floral tape.

10 Choose a colour for the flowers: I used White, Soft Lilac and Pale Pink SFP. Roll a tiny piece of SFP in your chosen colour into a ball. Glue the base of the pistil, push it through the paste and re-form into a small oval. Allow to dry.

Top tip

If the paste is large enough, make an extra petal to allow for breakages.

Petals

11 Grease a non-stick board with white vegetable fat. Roll out the paste fairly thinly, turn it over on a non-greased area of the board and cut out five petals using the larger cutter.

12 Use the veiner tool to texture the surface of the widest end of each petal and then soften the edges with a ball tool on a foam pad. Elongate the pointed end of the petal with the ball tool.

13 Make a further set of petals for the double Lisianthus using the same cutter.

14 Place the petals into a former or an apple tray so that the tops curl backwards until they hold their shape.

Top tip

It is important to use edible glue very sparingly when assembling this flower.

Assembling the Flower

15 Brush the base of the petals with a little edible glue and stick them together in a fan shape.

16 Brush some glue onto the oval shape below the pistil/stamens and gently wrap the fanned petals around this, making sure they curl around evenly. The oval shape should not be visible if possible as it is only there to help with the attachment of the petals and for support. Squeeze the petals together gently at the base.

17 For a double lisianthus, brush some edible glue on the bottom of a petal and stick it over a join between the inner petals. Continue to add the second layer of petals, overlapping the petals around the flower. Squeeze the base together and curl the petals back.

18 Place the flower into a former to firm, then dust the edges of the petals with a darker colour if required: I have used Lilac Dust Food Colour.

Calyx

19 The calyx of this flower is very fine and wispy and therefore I have chosen to make it with floral tape. Cut a 6cm (2½") length of ½-width light green floral tape and cut it into pieces down the length. Make five for each flower. Cut one end into a point and twist it into a strand, leaving a wider base.

20 Place the wide end against the petal and taped stem, press gently and twist it around the stem to hold it in place. Repeat this around the flower.

21 Tape over the calyx around the base of the flower with ½-width tape and continue down the stem.

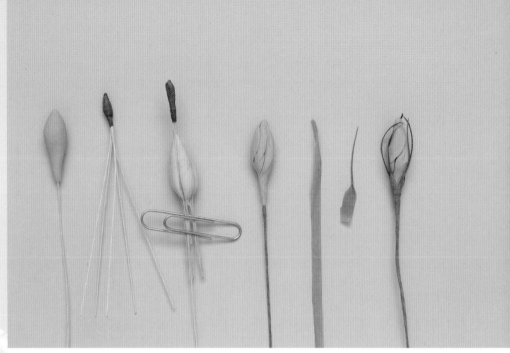

Buds

22   Make a cage with five pieces of 26-gauge wire (see page 18).

23   Form a small, pointed cone of SFP in your chosen colour, measuring approximately 2.5cm (1") long, and place this into the cage. Squeeze the cage gently to push the paste out between the wires. Hold the wires in place with a paper clip.

24   Use a pair of tweezers to squeeze the paste, flattening the paste further whilst still held in the cage. Remove the cage and pinch the flattened paste again with your fingers, then gently twist and wrap it round itself in a cone shape. Allow to dry.

25   Make the calyx as per the flower and attach it onto the bud. Cut the wisps to size as required. Tape the flower stem with ¼-width light green floral tape.

26   Make a few smaller, green buds in varying sizes; you will not need to use the cage technique but instead, mark

five lines from the bottom to the top with a craft knife then twist the bud into a spiral. Add a calyx as before.

27   Tape down the wire with ¼-width light green floral tape. The buds grow on long stems so do not cut the wire off.

Leaves

28   Cut a 28-gauge green wire into three equal lengths.

29   Mix a small amount of Holly/Ivy SFP with some Edelweiss SFP to make a soft, greyish colour.

30   Roll out the paste and cut out the leaves either freehand or using the templates, then follow your chosen method for wiring the leaves (see pages 19 to 22).

31   Vein the leaves with a Dresden tool and soften the edges with a ball tool. Dust the leaves with a little Leaf Green Dust Food Colour.

32   The leaves grow in pairs down the stem and each stem has approximately

eight to 12 leaves, depending on the length. Repeat to make as many leaves as required then steam the leaves to set the colour.

Assembly

33 Tape a green bud with one or two coloured buds together onto a 20-gauge wire. Add a flower below these and a pair of leaves opposite each other. Continue taping down the stem, then add another flower and a pair of leaves.

34 Make another stem of buds and a flower and add a pair of leaves as before. Tape these to the main stem, then continue to add a bud and two more pairs of leaves.

35 Repeat the process with flowers and buds in another colour to make a similar stem.

Top tip Leave the stems of the buds and flowers long.

For the Arrangement

3 white flowers

3 lilac flowers

1 pink flower

12 buds

30 leaves

Blossom plunger cutters (PME)

Butterfly paper punch

5 square miniature cakes covered in sugarpaste (see pages 168 to 172) and decorated with tiny blossoms, paper punched butterflies, piping and edible glitter

Tall, silver vase for single flower

This piece has been designed especially as a gift and a keepsake, perhaps to stand beside a cake decorated with a spray of similar flowers.

Put some sugarpaste/pastillage into the vase to hold the flowers in position. Place two stems of lisianthus into the vase at different heights.

Place each mini cake onto a cake card of the same size and cover with sugarpaste in the same way as for a large cake. Use a tiny blossom plunger cutter to make the flowers and secure them to the sides of the cakes with a dot of royal icing. Pipe the centres with white royal icing and add a line of beading around the tops of the cakes. Make tiny butterflies from White SFP using a paper punch and allow to dry on a former before attaching to the cakes with edible glue. Sprinkle the cakes with edible glitter flakes.

Surround the base of the vase with the little cakes and place a flower beside them to complete the display.

Cake Presentation

If you are displaying sugar flowers on a cake for a special occasion, you will need to think about how the cake is to be presented. Choose a shape and colour scheme to complement the flowers and make sure the cake is the right size for the number of guests. (You can always use an extra cutting cake if necessary.)

I have presented some of the flowers in this book on cakes and have suggested shapes, sizes and colours for the cakes, but you can, of course, choose your own design to suit the occasion. Others are displayed in a vase but would look equally stunning on a cake for a special occasion.

Cake size and shape	Quantity of marzipan and/or sugarpaste
15cm (6") round	450g (1lb)
20.5cm (8") round	800g (1¾lb)
25.5cm (10") round	1.13kg (2½lb)
15cm (6") square	680g (1½lb)
20.5cm (8") square	970g (2lb 2oz)
25.5cm (10") square	1.36kg (3lb)
15cm (6") heart	450g (1lb)
20.5cm (8") heart	700g (1lb 9oz)
25.5cm (10") heart	1kg (2lb 3oz)

The quantity of paste required to cover a cake will vary depending on the depth of the cake, so use of this chart is only intended as a guide.

How to Cover a Cake

Materials

Buttercream and jam (for a sponge cake) or marzipan, clear alcohol and apricot jam (for a fruitcake)

Cooled, boiled water

Icing sugar

Royal icing (small amount, optional)

Sugarpaste (available in ready-to-use packs from your local sugarcraft shop, see suppliers on page 176)

Equipment

Kitchen paper

Non-stick board

Non-toxic glue stick or double-sided tape

Plastic dowelling rods

15mm width ribbon in your choice of colour

Rolling pin

Scriber/glass-headed pin

Smoother

Small, sharp knife

Spacers (optional)

Turntable (optional)

Preparing the Cake

Clean the cake drum (board) with kitchen paper dampened with clear alcohol or cooled, boiled water and allow to air dry.

Rich fruit cake

1 To prepare a rich fruit cake for the marzipan and sugarpaste coating, make a sausage of marzipan and place this around the top edge, sticking it in place with apricot jam.

2 Invert the cake to give a flat, even surface on the top and place it onto a cake drum that is at least 8cm-10cm (3"-4") larger than the cake. If you are using a fruitcake, use pieces of marzipan to fill in any holes in the cake and the gap around the bottom edge. Ensure the surface is smooth, then brush apricot jam over the surface of the cake.

3 Cover the cake with a layer of marzipan, following the method for the sugarpaste covering overleaf. Allow the marzipan to firm, preferably overnight,

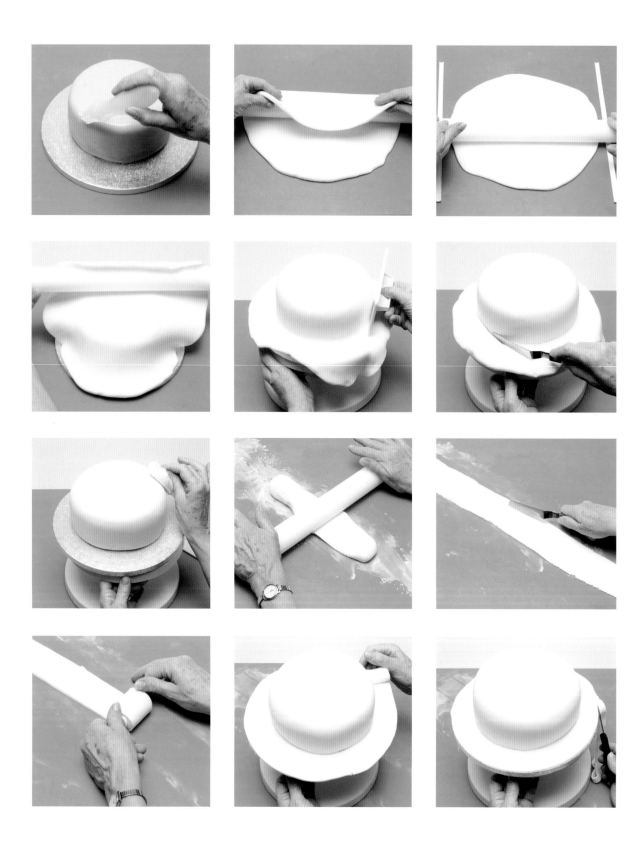

then brush with clear alcohol (such as gin or vodka) or cooled, boiled water to dampen the marzipan surface and help the sugarpaste to stick.

Sponge cake

If you are using a sponge cake, cut the top flat and invert it. Place it onto a cake drum that is at least 8cm-10cm (3"-4") larger than the cake. Fill it with jam and/ or buttercream then crumb-coat the surface of the cake with a thin layer of jam or buttercream to seal the cake.

Covering the Cake

1 Knead the sugarpaste until soft and pliable. You may need to dust a little icing sugar onto the work surface if the paste starts to stick to it at this stage.

2 Measure the top and sides of the cake to determine how large the sugarpaste will need to be when rolled out.

3 Dust the work surface with a small amount of icing sugar (do not use too much as it will dry out the paste). Roll out the sugarpaste, rotating the paste by ¼ turn frequently to ensure it is not sticking and is an even, round shape. Do not turn the paste over. The paste needs to be approximately 5mm (¼") thick for a smooth covering; rolling the paste out between spacers is helpful as this ensures it is an even thickness.

4 Flip the sugarpaste over the rolling pin towards you and lift it up to the prepared cake. (Using the rolling pin to transfer the paste to the cake minimises the risk of marking the paste with your fingers.) Adjust the sugarpaste so the centre of the paste is roughly in the centre of the cake top then gently place it onto the cake top.

5 Smooth the top surface with a smoother, removing any air bubbles from under the paste. Working gradually and evenly around the sides of the cake, ease the paste into place with the palm of your hand, starting at the corners if applicable. Smooth out any pleats and use your other hand to lift the edges of the paste as you work to prevent the paste from tearing along the top edge.

6 Use both hands to smooth the sugarpaste and press it onto the sides of the cake, turning the cake frequently to ensure that the covering is even. Gently rub a smoother over the top and sides of the cake to create a completely smooth surface.

Top tip

Placing the cake onto a turntable at this stage will make it much easier to work on.

7 Cut the excess sugarpaste away from the base of the cake using a sharp knife, then gently smooth the surfaces with the palm of your hand.

8 Finally, use a smoother or a pad of sugarpaste covered in cling film to smooth and buff the covering one last time.

Covering the Cake Drum
(Board)

There are several ways to cover a cake board, so choose whichever you prefer.

Method 1: Bandage method

1 Place the covered cake in the centre of the cake drum (board).

2 Roll a sausage of sugarpaste to the approximate length of the exposed board around the edge of the cake.

3 Cut a straight edge at either end of the sausage then lightly dust the work surface with icing sugar and gently roll to widen and lengthen the paste. Once the sugarpaste is approximately 5mm (¼") thick, cut a straight edge along one side to approximately the width of the exposed board and lightly dust the surface with icing sugar. Roll up the sugarpaste into a coil.

4 Brush a little cooled, boiled water on the cake board around the edge of the cake, then with a damp paintbrush, dampen under the outer edge of the sugarpaste. Carefully unroll the sugarpaste around the board, easing the straight edge up to the base of the covered cake.

5 Cut through the paste at the join and remove any excess pieces. Smooth the surface of the paste with a smoother.

6 Trim away the excess paste to neaten the edge. Allow to dry.

7 To give the cake a professional finish, trim the edge of the cake drum with ribbon. Measure the drum then cut a length of ribbon 2.5cm (1") longer. Use a non-toxic glue stick or double-sided tape to secure the ribbon in place, ensuring that the join is at the back of the cake. If you are using a glue stick, make sure it does not come into contact with the sugarpaste covering.

Method 2: Pre-covered board

1 Brush the cake drum with clear alcohol or cooled, boiled water then cover the cake board with sugarpaste. Smooth over the surface with a smoother and trim neatly around the sides. Finish with ribbon, as described above.

2 Place the cake onto a thin cake board of the same size and cover it in the usual way. Once the board covering is firm, place the cake in position and secure in place with royal icing or thick sugar glue made from sugarpaste and edible glue.

Method 3: All-in-one method

1 Place the cake onto the cake drum and follow the instructions for preparing the cake.

2 Roll out the sugarpaste, ensuring that it is large enough to cover the cake and the exposed cake drum around it.

3 Dampen the exposed cake drum with cooled, boiled water or clear alcohol then cover the cake and drum all-in-one. Smooth the top and sides of the cake then the cake drum, ensuring that the paste is at 90° to the cake sides. (This ensures that any ribbon or decorations that you may wish to use will sit neatly around the cake.) Trim off any excess paste from around the edge.

Stacking Cakes

1 Place the upper tiers onto thin cake boards of the same size then cover the cakes on the boards as previously described, ensuring the boards cannot be seen. Cover the base tier and the drum as previously described. Allow the sugarpaste to harden for a few hours then dowel and stack the cakes before the sugarpaste dries completely.

2 Make a template the same size and shape as the cake/s to be stacked. Place the template onto the surface of the lower tier and lightly mark where the next tier is to be positioned, using a scriber or glass-headed pin to indent the sugarpaste surface.

3 Push between four and six plastic dowelling rods (depending on the weight of the cake to be supported) within the marked area on the base tier. The denser the cake and the more tiers you use, the more dowels you will need.

4 Use a pencil to mark each dowel where it meets the surface of the cake then remove them from the cake. Make sure the pencil does not come into contact with the sugarpaste.

5 Line the dowels up against each other, ensuring the bases are level, then place a ruler across them, level with the highest point marked on the dowels. Score across this line with a craft knife then trim the dowels to the same height.

6 Reposition the dowels in the cake with the cut end uppermost. Spread a small amount of royal icing between the dowels to show clearly where they are in the cake. This will enable caterers or those cutting the cake to see the dowels easily and remove them safely before the cake is cut.

7 Repeat this process until all the cakes (except the top tier) are dowelled, then carefully stack the cake from the base upwards. Leave the cakes for approximately 24 hours, allowing the paste to set off.

NB: It is advisable to inform the recipient/caterers that they must remove all the dowels (as well as any other inedible items such as ribbon and posy picks) before cutting the cake.

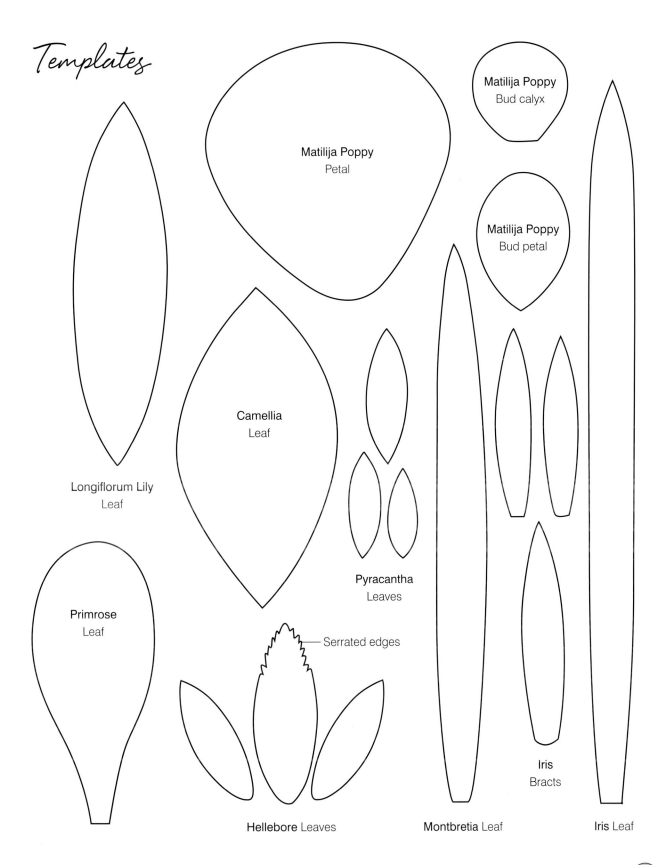

Templates

Matilija Poppy
Petal

Matilija Poppy
Bud calyx

Matilija Poppy
Bud petal

Longiflorum Lily
Leaf

Camellia
Leaf

Pyracantha
Leaves

Primrose
Leaf

Serrated edges

Iris
Bracts

Hellebore Leaves

Montbretia Leaf

Iris Leaf

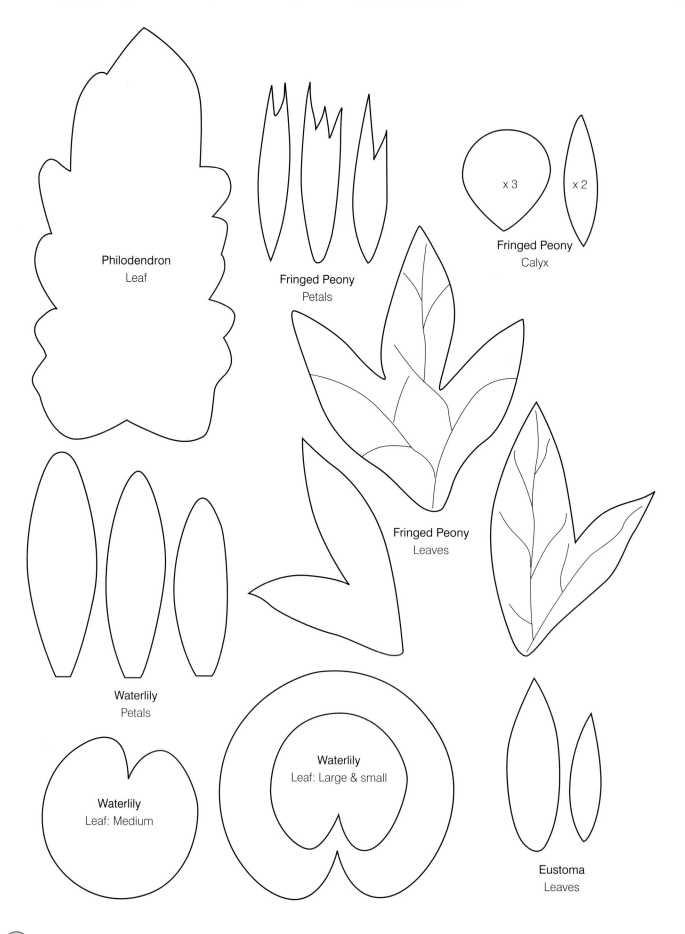

Philodendron
Leaf

Fringed Peony
Petals

Fringed Peony
Calyx

x 3   x 2

Fringed Peony
Leaves

Waterlily
Petals

Waterlily
Leaf: Large & small

Waterlily
Leaf: Medium

Eustoma
Leaves

Index

Suppliers

Squires Kitchen

Squires Kitchen, UK

Squires House
3 Waverley Lane
Farnham
Surrey
GU9 8BB
0845 61 71 810
+44 (0) 1252 260 260
www.squires-shop.com

Squires Kitchen International School

The Grange
Hones Yard
Farnham
Surrey
GU9 8BB
0845 61 71 812
+44 (0) 1252 260 262
www.squires-school.co.uk

Squires Kitchen, France

+33 (0) 1 82 88 01 66
clientele@squires-shop.fr
www.squires-shop.fr

Squires Kitchen, Spain

+34 93 180 7382
cliente@squires-shop.es
www.squires-shop.es

Shops

UK

Decor 4 Cakes Ltd.
Essex
+44 (0)1255 422 031

Jane Asher Party Cakes
London
www.jane-asher.co.uk

Canada

SugarTiers Inc.
Ontario
www.sugartiers.ca

Greece

Sugar World - Aliprantis Ltd.
Athens
www.sugarworld.gr

Italy

Maison Madeleine
www.maisonmadeleine.it

Malaysia

International Centre of Cake
Artistry Sdn. Bhd.
Selangor
www.2decoratecakes.com

Nigeria

Kogsy Merchandise
Lagos
www.kogsycakeandsugarcraft.com

Poland

Tortownia
Warszawa
www.tortownia.pl

Sweden

Tårtdecor
Kungälv
www.tartdecor.se

USA

Beryl's Cake Decorating and
Pastry Supplies
N. Springfield, VA
www.beryls.com

Distributors

UK

Confectionery Supplies
Herefordshire
www.confectionerysupplies.co.uk

Culpitt Ltd.
Northumberland
www.culpitt.com

Guy, Paul & Co. Ltd.
Buckinghamshire
www.guypaul.co.uk

Australia

Zoratto Enterprises
New South Wales
+61 (2) 9457 0009

New Zealand

See Zoratto Enterprises,
Australia

Manufacturers

UK

AP Cutters (AP)
Weston-super-Mare
+44 (0)1934 812 787

CelCakes & CelCrafts
York
www.celcrafts.co.uk

Fine Cut Sugarcraft
Nottingham
www.finecutsugarcraft.com

FMM Sugarcraft
Hertfordshire
www.fmmsugarcraft.com

Food Packaging &
Cakeboards Ltd.
Lancashire
www.fpcb.co.uk

Holly Products (HP)
Cheshire
www.hollyproducts.co.uk

Knightsbridge PME Ltd.
Middlesex
www.cakedecoration.co.uk

Orchard Products
East Sussex
www.orchardproducts.co.uk

Patchwork Cutters
Merseyside
www.patchworkcutters.co.uk

Smeg UK Ltd.
www.smeguk.com
www.smeg50style.com
Italian appliance manufacturer
Smeg produce distinctive
domestic appliances combining
design, performance and quality.

Squires Kitchen Trade
0845 61 71 813
+44 (0) 1252 260 263

Tinkertech Two (TT) – see
Confectionery Supplies

South Africa

JEM Cutters (JC)
Kloof
www.jemcutters.com

Guilds

The British Sugarcraft Guild
London
www.bsguk.org